Contents

KT-226-543

Alister Ross

NEW PLAYS 1

GENERAL EDITOR
Peter Terson

Activities section by
Steve Barlow and Steve Skidmore

Oxford University Press 1988

Oxford University Press, Walton Street, Oxford OX2 6DP

Oxford New York Toronto
Delhi Bombay Calcutta Madras Karachi
Petaling Jaya Singapore Hong Kong Tokyo
Nairobi Dar es Salaam Cape Town
Melbourne Auckland

and associated companies in
Berlin Ibadan

Oxford is a trade mark of Oxford University Press

© This arrangement Peter Terson

ISBN 019 8312563

Typeset by Pentacor Ltd, High Wycombe, Bucks
Printed in Great Britain by
Richard Clay Ltd, Bungay, Suffolk

Acknowledgements

The publishers thank the authors and their agents listed below for
permission to publish the plays in this volume.

How to Write a Play and The Weeping Madonna © Peter Terson.
Application for performance should be made to Sales and Marketing
Services, Cathedral House, Beacon St., Lichfield, Staffs. WS13 7AA.

Little Old Lady © Arnold Wesker. Application for performance should
be made to NJ Media Enterprises Ltd, 10 Clorane Gardens,
London NW3 7 PR.

The Great Camel Rumbles and Groans and Spits © Henry Livings.
Application for performance should be made to Harvey Unna and
Stephen Durbridge Ltd, 24 Pottery Lane, London W11 4LZ.

A Slight Hitch © Juliet Ace.

Slave! © Myles Eckersley.

A Message From The Other Side © Joyce Holliday.

The Pressure-Cooker © Steve Barlow and Steve Skidmore.

Application for performance of A Slight Hitch, Slave!, A Message From
The Other Side and The Pressure-Cooker should be made
to Oxford University Press.

Introduction

When I was asked by Oxford University Press to prepare an anthology of one act plays for schools I wrote off to a number of playwrights I'd known personally, or heard of professionally, and then waited.

Half of them didn't answer and this was the worst reply of all.

Some said they didn't have an idea in their heads and this was the most honest reply of all.

Some said that they had an old piece 'lying around that might do' and this was the most slovenly reply of all.

And then, the important few said that they would love to try it, and this was the most heartening reply of all.

Soon, really vigorous, fresh work began to come in.

Among them there was a feeling of excitement. It was as if the playwrights could say things in a one-act play that could be said no other way. It was as if they were addressing their audience more directly than usual, stepping into the classroom to speak to them.

So I hope they work, and as apart from A Slight Hitch none of these plays has been performed before, you can have a World Premiere. I'm sure some of the authors would love to be invited along, (I know I would), and if you ask very nicely Henry Livings might play the camel.

Peter Terson

HOW TO WRITE A PLAY
PETER TERSON

Characters

COLIN

IAN

GIRL

TOUGH

I wrote this play for a bit of fun really. I wanted to demonstrate how the bits and pieces of everyday life form a drama.

I tried to show, humorously, how a play is UNFOLDING around two boys without them being the slightest bit aware of it.

'All the World's a Stage,' Shakespeare said resignedly, and so it is, and it's the playwright's job (and gift), to reveal the play of life to others.

If this sounds pompous, read the play.

> *A canal or river bank.*
> COLIN *and* IAN *come along loaded up with fishing gear.*

COLIN How will this spot do you?
IAN Fine.
COLIN Are you *sure*?

IAN Yes.

COLIN Are you sure you're sure?

IAN I'm sure, I'm sure I'm sure.

COLIN Right.

IAN Right.

COLIN You won't change your mind?

IAN Course I won't change my mind.

COLIN You won't think it's better, for example, over there, under the withies, or along there by that boat?

IAN Course I won't.

COLIN This is fine then? By you?

IAN Fine.

COLIN Right.

IAN Right then.

[*They start to set up.*]

COLIN Now, before I fit this rod up, you are happy here?

IAN Yes. Fit it up.

COLIN And before I fit on this reel you're not going to change your mind?

IAN Fit it on, fit it on.

[COLIN *fits up. Sits down.*]

COLIN We can now prepare for a serious solace.

IAN Suits me.

COLIN No jumping about, no getting restless, no fidgeting.

IAN How I like it. I saw one jump under the withies.

COLIN Forget it.

IAN Forgot.

COLIN [*After a while*] You know what we've got for our English homework?

IAN No. What?

COLIN Write a play.

IAN Flipping heck.

COLIN That's what I said.

IAN A play!

COLIN A play, a short one.

IAN How short?

COLIN Five minutes.

IAN Flipping heck.

COLIN Or longer.

IAN Longer!

COLIN Like six minutes.

IAN You could run a mile in six minutes.

COLIN What's that got to do with it?

IAN Well you can do a lot in six minutes.

COLIN People say a lot in six minutes.

IAN A single runs for four minutes.

COLIN Well, I've got to write a play that runs five minutes . . . but I might get away with four minutes. Does this suit you here?

IAN Yes.

COLIN What you fidgeting for then?

IAN I'm not fidgeting.

COLIN Bags I first in.

IAN Why should you be?

COLIN 'Cos I bagged it.

IAN I want to be first in.

COLIN Look at that cloud formation of cumulus nimbus.

IAN *looks up*. COLIN *casts in*.

IAN That wasn't fair.

COLIN Just testing.

IAN Testing what?

COLIN Your competitive spirit.

IAN I wanted to be in last anyway; the fish always swim away from the first cast.

Pause.

IAN How do you go about it then?

COLIN Go about what?

IAN Writing a play.

COLIN Oh that!

IAN You don't know.

COLIN I do know. First of all you need a *setting*.

IAN A setting?

COLIN A place to set it in.

IAN That's hard.

COLIN It could be anywhere. A simple setting.

IAN Like where?

COLIN Anywhere, it could be just a bit of fence, patch of artificial grass, a tree stump.

He is describing where they are.

It's like to set the scene for actors to be in. Setting.

IAN Actors are always in settings aren't they?
Ordinary people aren't; it never happens to the likes of us.

COLIN It could be anywhere.

IAN But anywhere isn't a *real setting*.
A real setting is a jungle, or New York or the prairie, that's a real setting.

COLIN How much ground-bait do you think you're putting down?

IAN I want to attract them.

COLIN Attract them! You'll overcrowd them.

IAN Hi, look at them.

COLIN What?

IAN The maggots, all writhing and struggling in their tin.

COLIN They keep busy.

IAN All that effort to be bred and born just to be put on a hook to feed to fish.

COLIN It's like life itself. Are you getting restless?

IAN What do you mean?

COLIN You seem unsettled. Would you rather fish somewhere else?

IAN No, I'm settled.

COLIN Good.

IAN It suits me.

COLIN Great.

IAN It's just that the fish seem *more active* over there.

COLIN It's just an illusion.

[*Pause.*]

IAN What do you do next?

COLIN When?

IAN Writing a play. Once you've got your scene set, like in the jungle, New York, the prairies . . .

COLIN Or here.

IAN What do you do next?

COLIN Then you introduce the *persona dramatis*.

IAN Who are they?

COLIN Characters.

IAN Flipping heck.

COLIN That's what I said.

IAN What do they do?

COLIN Indulge in dialogue.

IAN What!

COLIN Talk.

IAN Cripes.

COLIN Well said.

IAN What will they talk about?

COLIN The teacher said 'just listen to other people' and put it in.

IAN But that's eavesdropping.

COLIN No, it's eavesdropping if you're just listening. But if you're listening to put it in writing that's listening, not eavesdropping.

IAN People never say anything worth listening to anyway do they? They just boss you about, snap at you, snarl; they never say anything interesting.

COLIN That is the dilemma of the playwright.

Pause.

IAN Those maggots are eternally restless.

COLIN Like life itself.

IAN Do you know what the funniest thing I ever heard about maggots was?

COLIN No, what?

IAN These two anglers went out fishing on a frosty morning.

COLIN Where?

IAN What?

COLIN Where did they go? Canal? River? Lake? Sea? Pond?

IAN What does that matter?

COLIN I'm trying to set the scene.

IAN Lake then.

COLIN Right.

IAN They went fishing and they were using maggots.

COLIN What sort of maggots?

IAN The general commercial maggot.

COLIN They didn't breed their own?

IAN Not as far as I know.

COLIN So they weren't *professional* anglers?

IAN They were pretty good.

COLIN But not all *that* good.

IAN Pretty good mate; they were out fishing early on a frosty morning.

COLIN But they didn't breed their own maggots.

[*Pause.*]

COLIN Go on.

IAN I think they *did* breed their own maggots.

COLIN Make your mind up, I'm trying to define the characters.

IAN Anyway, as it was cold, the maggots were a bit sluggish, so one of the anglers put them in his mouth to keep warm.

COLIN He *was* a professional.

IAN However, some of his breakfast was still between his teeth.

COLIN What was it?

IAN Bacon and that. And they *fed* off it . . . and he started catching lots of fish.

COLIN Because the maggots were so succulent.

IAN I suppose so, and this annoyed his mate so much that he *pushed him.*

COLIN Playfully?

IAN Off his stool, but his mouth was full of maggots and he swallowed them.

COLIN Still alive?

IAN And breeding fast. But they fished on.

COLIN How long for?

IAN Till mid morning, when the sun came out. Then they went home.

COLIN By car?

IAN Yeah.

COLIN Whose car?

IAN Is it important whose car it was?

COLIN It is to me, I'm trying to conjure up the picture.

IAN It was the car of the other man.

COLIN The one who didn't swallow the maggots?

IAN Yes. And he dropped his friend off at home. But when he got in the house he fell down the stairs and broke his neck.

COLIN He must have been wearing his boots.

IAN He was, and as he lived alone they didn't find him for *three days*, and when he *did* find him he was dead but still moving.

COLIN Reflexes?

IAN Maggots.

> *They fish on philosophically.*

IAN Now that's the sort of dialogue you couldn't put in a play.

COLIN I wouldn't want to?

IAN Why?

COLIN It doesn't further the plot.

IAN The plot?

COLIN The story.

IAN What plot does it have to have?

COLIN Anything.

IAN Murder? Gangsters? Fire, cowboys, mutiny, space wars and that.

COLIN Anything. It could be about anything. Or nothing.

IAN You can't have a play about nothing.

COLIN Shakespeare did, Much Ado About Nothing.

IAN You couldn't do it twice.

COLIN It could be about a person, like Hamlet.

IAN Superman.

COLIN Mother Courage.

IAN Toad of Toad Hall.

COLIN Or it could be about a journey, like, Pilgrim's Progress.

IAN From Here to Eternity.

COLIN The Long March.

IAN Bus-stop.

COLIN Or it could be about the *end* of a journey, like Journey's End.

IAN Or Bus-stop.

COLIN You said Bus-stop before.

IAN There are lots of bus-stops on a journey.

COLIN You want to move don't you?

IAN I didn't say that.

COLIN You're not happy fishing here.

IAN I'm OK.

COLIN You'd rather fish over there.

IAN No.

COLIN You've got no patience.

IAN I'm as patient as you and I'll prove it.

COLIN How?

IAN First one to say he wants to pack in is impatient, OK?

COLIN OK.

IAN What else do you need in your play?

COLIN Tension.

IAN Can't help you.

They sit.
IAN *takes out his thermos.*

COLIN Coffee already?

IAN Any objections?

COLIN Just wondering.

IAN Wonder to yourself.

COLIN You'll be having a biscuit, I suppose.

IAN Might.

COLIN And a slab of Mum's fruit-cake?

IAN Mind your own business.

COLIN Then your sandwiches?

IAN We'll see.

COLIN The worst of coming out with you is that you
bring enough food to last all day, then by eleven
o'clock you've eaten it all and you want to pack in
and go home.

IAN I don't.

COLIN You do.

IAN Do you want to pack in?

COLIN No.

IAN Just testing.

Pause.

COLIN Don't throw your crumbs into the water; it
spoils the delicate balance of my bait.

IAN Where will you get your plot from then?

COLIN Life.

IAN But nothing happens in life.

COLIN There are births, and deaths. And life in
between.

IAN But not *plots* . . . It's amazing how *nothing* can
happen in life. I mean, look at my Mum and Dad.

COLIN I'd rather not.

IAN Nothing has happened to them at all. They just sit and watch telly night after night. Not a plot in sight.

COLIN Perhaps they're seething with inner drama.

IAN They can't be, they don't *do anything*.

COLIN But they went to London that time.

IAN That was just for Dad's interview.

COLIN For that job he didn't get.

IAN He was offered it but Mum didn't want to move.

COLIN Because of Gran.

IAN She felt responsible; she didn't want to move Gran.

COLIN Then Gran died.

IAN And Dad reapplied for the job.

COLIN But it was filled.

IAN Filled.

COLIN Then his old job was made redundant.

IAN And him and Mum had a row.

COLIN So your Vera ran away from home and married an unsuitable chap.

IAN And Mum followed her to Canada.

COLIN And Dad got out his old motor bike.

IAN To rebuild it.

COLIN His first love.

IAN The Velocette.

COLIN Then Mum came home.

IAN Because Vera's husband left.

COLIN And Dad never finished rebuilding his motor bike.

IAN Because Mum didn't like it in the front room.

COLIN So he sold it for spare parts then discovered later . . .

IAN It was a valuable antique . . . but that's not drama.

COLIN My teacher Binnie Moffat says there's drama in everything.

IAN She's a spinster though.

COLIN And when you feel it's getting static you introduce a new character.

> *Enter* GIRL *and stands behind them.*

IAN Who do you introduce?

COLIN Anybody. Because a three-sided situation is more interesting than a two-sided.

IAN Is it?

COLIN Yes. It makes it more three dimensional.

IAN How?

COLIN Well, when there's *three characters* there's more *inter relationship*.

IAN What will the other character be doing?

COLIN I don't know . . . the other character can be doing *nothing* . . . just *standing* there.

IAN That's a bit boring.

COLIN If a new character came between your Mum and Dad and just *stood* there it would be more interesting.

IAN Be incredible.

COLIN It produces a new interplay of relationships.

IAN It would produce a heart attack in our house.

> *Pause.*

IAN What do you think *she* wants?

COLIN Dunno.

IAN If we say nothing she might go away.

> GIRL *sighs deeply.*

COLIN Do you want to move?

IAN You always think I want to move.

COLIN I mean, do you want to move if *somebody's* spoiling it . . .

IAN That *somebody* might go.

COLIN When do you think that *somebody* might go?

IAN Depends what that *somebody* is here for.

COLIN We could ask.

IAN You ask, you're supposed to have the enquiring mind.

COLIN But you're nosiest . . .

IAN Are you out for a walk?

GIRL *goes off.*

IAN Charming, that didn't tell us much.

COLIN It told us a great deal.

IAN Such as?

COLIN For a start she's got something on her mind.

IAN Brilliant.

COLIN And . . . she comes from the council estate.

IAN How do you know?

COLIN The mud on her shoes is from over there. And she slipped out of the house without breakfast.

IAN How do you make that out?

COLIN She had a packet of biscuits in her hand.

IAN She might have come to feed the ducks.

COLIN Not with chocolate biscuits, especially as she's running away.

IAN Go on . . .

COLIN She's heavily clothed and her eyes are red, but she's thought about it carefully.

IAN How do you know that?

COLIN She's put her make-up on with great care. And now she's in a state of indecision.

IAN How do you know?

COLIN Because she's stopped again.

IAN So she has.

COLIN She's looking into the water.

IAN Contemplating suicide?

COLIN No.

IAN How do you know that?

COLIN She's got a new magazine. No girl would drown herself without reading her magazine first.

IAN She might be waiting for some bloke.

COLIN No she isn't.

IAN How are you so certain?

COLIN She hasn't looked at her watch. All girls look at their watch when they're waiting for a bloke.

IAN You're too clever.

COLIN I know but I fight it. Would you be quiet now please?

IAN What for?

COLIN I'm occupied.

IAN What by?

COLIN The Muse.

IAN Who's that?

COLIN The God of the Muse, helping me to write this play.

IAN Do you need a God for that?

COLIN Certainly . . . 'Let me in Laurel leaves be crowned.'

IAN Jese.

COLIN There's something missing.

IAN What is it?

COLIN Suspense.

IAN Suspense!

COLIN That's what you need in a play, suspense.

IAN Like, holding your breath?

COLIN Yes, like that.

IAN A cliff-hanger?

COLIN Like that. It usually comes from an external
force . . .

IAN Like from the outer galaxies?

COLIN Or nearer.

⌈   *Enter* TOUGH.   ⌉

TOUGH You fishing?

COLIN That's an inspired observation.

IAN Yes, we're fishing.

TOUGH Nothing better to do with your lives?

COLIN We study *philosophy* too.

IAN We like fishing.

TOUGH What if I say you *can't*?

COLIN We'd be tempted to question your authority.

IAN We'd ask you to let us.

TOUGH Is this box important to you anglers?

COLIN No, we brought it for show.

IAN Yes, it's full of our tackle.

TOUGH [*Putting his foot to box*] What if I was to push
it in the canal?

COLIN It would result in a splash.

IAN Please don't.

TOUGH I better inspect your fishing licences.

COLIN We don't show them to lesser species.

IAN Here's mine.

TOUGH [*To* COLIN] You, I might be back for you.

⌈   *He goes.*   ⌉

IAN He might be back for you.

COLIN So he said.

IAN What'll you do?

COLIN Whether 'tis more noble to stand and wait possible annihilation, or take resolve and courage from the situation.

IAN He's going to that girl.

COLIN Step by step. Note how he goes.

IAN How does he go?

COLIN Undecidedly.

IAN Undecidedly?

COLIN He's an indecisive person. He can't even decide which line his mischief will take . . .

IAN He's approaching her!

COLIN Indeed he is.

IAN Her back is to him.

COLIN She is unaware.

IAN He might push her in.

COLIN A possibility.

IAN Or abuse her.

COLIN Verbally he is limited.

IAN He might even assault her . . .

COLIN In a frenzy of . . .

IAN He might haul her into the bushes and . . .

COLIN Rape.

IAN God, what will we do? I can't look. The nearer he gets. I can't decide . . . We must do something? But what . . . is he there? Tell me the worst.

COLIN He's past her unharmed.

IAN Thank God for that. [*Recovering*] I'd have killed him you know.

COLIN Would you?

IAN Oh yes. If he'd interfered with her I was resolved.

COLIN You hid it well.

IAN That's my calm exterior; underneath I was in a state of *ice-cold viciousness*.

COLIN That's interesting.

IAN My muscles were like tempered steel.

COLIN Good, he's coming back.

IAN What? I'm packing up. I'm getting out. You coming?

COLIN No, I'm thinking of my *deux ex machina*.

IAN What's that?

COLIN A *deux ex machina* is a contrived way of ending a play . . . like sudden flight.

IAN In that case I'm off . . . will you bring my rod?

COLIN Sure . . . hi Ian.

IAN What?

COLIN Your muscles of tempered steel have turned to jelly in your legs.

IAN *goes.*

Enter GIRL.

GIRL [*Sighs*] Can I talk to you?

COLIN If you want.

GIRL You see. I need advice. I'm undecided. I want to leave home . . . run away . . . I've found a room, and a job in a twine factory in another town . . . I mean . . . the world's open to me . . . but I'm afraid . . . I don't know whether to go on, or go back, I just can't make a decision. What do *you* think I should do?

Enter TOUGH.

COLIN Ask him, he has the same problem.

GIRL Excuse me . . . I need advice . . .

TOUGH Yeah?

GIRL You see I'm undecided . . . Let me tell you . . .
can I tell you?
TOUGH Sure.

> *They walk on.*
> *Re-enter* IAN.

IAN I've decided to come back.
COLIN I'm deep in thought.
IAN What about?
COLIN Writing a play. You see, I suppose some plays
need an *epilogue* . . . by way of explanation. An
afterthought, to explain hidden meanings. To tell the
audience the purpose of the play. Whether it was
finished, or that its life was going on. In a word, to
conclude it.
IAN I tell you what?
COLIN What?
IAN I think the fishing is hopeless here. I'd rather move
over there by the withies.
COLIN OK. I knew you'd get impatient first.
IAN You were impatient as well.
COLIN I wasn't.
IAN You were.
COLIN I wasn't.
IAN You were.
COLIN Wasn't.
IAN Were . . .

> *They go off with 'wasn't' and 'were'.*

LITTLE OLD LADY
ARNOLD WESKER

Characters

TRACY	aged 15
SAM	aged 15
LITTLE OLD LADY	aged 65
HARASSED WOMAN	aged 45
UNPLEASANT MAN	aged 19 or 50
JASON	aged 17

There will be six characters in this play. They can be white, African, Afro-Caribbean or Asian.

The choice will be that of the class or director or both. Changes of some words and rhythms may thus be necessary to suit whoever is chosen.

And here comes the first problem: who will be given which role? One character is less intelligent than another. Should a black student play it or a white? Does it matter? One character will be anti-social. Should a white student play it or an Asian? Does it matter? And who will play the heroine?

The problem arises because if a white student plays the anti-social character it will be understood that the play is simply saying *people* are anti-social; it is a fact of life not a racist statement. But if a black student plays the anti-social character it is interpreted as a statement about race not as a fact of life.

Should this be?

The play explores its own problem. How to mount the play presents another problem. It seemed worth identifying.

I wish only to point out that this play is not about race, and if chosen by a school with no black or Asian students, the dilemma will not arise.

Carriage of an underground train.

Sound of an underground train hurtling through its tube.

Lights up on interior of a London underground carriage. 'No Smoking' signs are in evidence.

Two young people sit side by side in the length-ways section. SAM *and* TRACY.

She is testing him from a diary full of information. It has been going on some time.

TRACY Capital of Spain?

SAM Dunno.

TRACY Madrid. Capital of Norway?

SAM Dunno.

TRACY Oslo. Capital of Italy?

SAM Dunno.

TRACY Rome.

SAM Oh, yeah! I knew that.

TRACY Capital of Finland?

SAM Sweden?

TRACY That's a country, dum-dum.

SAM You're right. Sweden's a country. What was I thinking of?

TRACY You weren't thinking.

SAM I was. I just made a mistake.

TRACY Capital of France?

SAM Er. I knew that one. I *know* I know that one.
It's – Berlin.

TRACY It's Paris.

SAM I meant Paris.

TRACY You didn't say Paris.

SAM You get mixed up, don't you? I mean they
mention cities all the time on telly but they don't tell
you where they are do they?

TRACY Well they can't keep saying 'The European
foreign ministers met today in Paris which, for those
of our viewers who don't know –

SAM – or 'ave forgotten –

TRACY – is in France.

SAM Why not?

TRACY Take too long wouldn't it?

SAM But it would educate us.

TRACY Television News is offered, dum-dum, on the
assumption that its viewers are already educated.

SAM Well they're wrong, ain't they?

TRACY Capital of Greece?

SAM Dunno.

TRACY Athens. Capital of Japan?

SAM Dunno.

TRACY Tokyo. Capital of Russia?

SAM [*jubilantly*] Moscow!

TRACY Right! Bloody right! Congratulations! Flaming
hallelujah! At last! Genius! Hero!

SAM Alright, alright. You'll give me a big 'ead.

TRACY Now that we know the capital of Russia can we
start having aitches where they belong? *H*ead. The
word is '*h*ead', not 'ead'.

SAM It's quicker to say 'bigead'. Say it like *you* want
and I've got to take a deep breath. Big [*breath*] *h*ead.

> *The train stops. Sound of doors opening.*
> *The* LITTLE OLD LADY *gets on.*

LITTLE OLD LADY Is this the right train for South
Kensington?

SAM [*Not looking at chart*] Yeah. You got King's
Cross, Russell Square, Holborn, Covent
Garden, Leicester Square, Piccadilly Circus,
Green Park, Hyde Park Corner, Knightsbridge
first. Then South Ken.

> *Sound of doors closing. Train moves off.*
> *She sits some seats away from them.*

TRACY Capital of Hungary?

SAM Dunno.

TRACY Budapest. Capital of Portugal?

SAM I don't even know where Portugal is.

TRACY Whereas you know where Hungary is, and
Finland and Norway?

SAM Don't be like that.

TRACY Well I am like that. You want to be my friend
you must take me like that.

SAM Cor! Girls ain't 'alf bossy.

TRACY [*Bossily*] That's sexist.

SAM Alright, *you're* bossy then.

TRACY That's better. Here. [*showing him map*]
Portugal.

SAM [*As though it's just come to him*] Lisbon.

TRACY You saw.

SAM I never. Print's too small.

TRACY Capital of New Zealand?

SAM Cor! You're getting really difficult, aren't you?

LITTLE OLD LADY You don't know the capital of New Zealand?

TRACY He doesn't know the capital of anywhere, missus.

LITTLE OLD LADY It's Wellington. Don't they teach you these things in school?

TRACY Got no time to teach us. Too busy getting us through exams.

LITTLE OLD LADY I don't think I understand that. Subtle.

SAM What's she on about? 'Subtle'?

TRACY Subtle, dum-dum, means the meaning isn't obvious [*To* LITTLE OLD LADY] It's simple, missus. They show us the kind of question we'll get in our exams and we just learn an assortment of answers.

LITTLE OLD LADY You don't seem stupid to me.

TRACY My dad's a civil servant isn't he, so I read books don't I!

LITTLE OLD LADY And your boyfriend doesn't?

TRACY He's not my boyfriend, he's the new next-door neighbour, and he's nicer than me.

LITTLE OLD LADY You mean people who read books are unpleasant, and people who don't read books are all honey and spice and everything nice?

TRACY I didn't say that.

LITTLE OLD LADY What's your names?

TRACY I'm Tracy he's Sam.

SAM I'm Sam she's Tracy.

LITTLE OLD LADY And I'm just an interfering old woman.

SAM Old? You're not old. Who says you're old?

LITTLE OLD LADY I think you're making fun of me. Don't young people think everyone over twenty-five is old?

SAM [*Taking book from* TRACY. *To* LITTLE OLD LADY]. Capital of Turkey?

LITTLE OLD LADY Ankara. Used to be Constantinople, now known as Istanbul. Istanbul! Dreary old sound. Constantinople's much nicer, don't you think? More romantic. Named after the Roman Emperor Constantine who was the first Roman Emperor to convert to Christianity you know. Started another Empire. The Byzantine. Now there's a romantic sound for you. Byzantine. Produced lots of paintings and churches. I used to love history at school. But I never saw anywhere. Couldn't afford to travel. Too late now.

SAM [*Hoping for another long answer*] Capital of China?

LITTLE OLD LADY Peking.

[*The young ones eagerly await.*]

I don't know anything about Chinese history.

SAM Capital of Mexico?

LITTLE OLD LADY Mexico City.

SAM Brazil?

LITTLE OLD LADY Brasilia.

SAM Peru?

LITTLE OLD LADY Lima.

SAM Nigeria?

LITTLE OLD LADY Lagos.

SAM Is there anywhere you don't know the capital of?

LITTLE OLD LADY I don't think I know the capital of – oh – Madagascar or the Fiji Isles, or, let me see now, Guinea-Bissau.

TRACY But she has *heard* of a place called Guinea Bissau. Have *you*, dum-dum?

> *Train stops. Sound of doors opening.*
> *Two people enter.*
>
> *The* HARASSED WOMAN *with cumbersome*
> *shopping, who sits.*
>
> *The* UNPLEASANT MAN, *who stands and sways.*
>
> *Sound of doors closing. Train moves off.*
> UNPLEASANT MAN *lights up a cigarette.*
> *Everyone watches. Mesmerised. No one says*
> *anything. They look at one another. Helpless.*
> *He's mean and aloof. Nothing and no one*
> *exists for him.*
>
> *The silence is long. Unease grows. He seems to*
> *flourish in such atmospheres.*
>
> *Finally –*

LITTLE OLD LADY Excuse me, sir, but smoking's not
permitted on the underground.

> *He glares at her, then ignores her.*
> *More silence.*

Well isn't anyone else going to say anything? No
support? Just one old lady?

> *The* HARASSED WOMAN *turns away, deeply*
> *embarrassed to be drawn into a public scene.*
>
> *The young ones take up their game, voices*
> *subdued now.*

SAM Capital of Egypt?
TRACY Cairo.
SAM Capital of Argentina?

TRACY Buenos Aires.
SAM Capital of South Africa?
TRACY Pretoria.
SAM Capital of USA?
UNPLEASANT MAN New York.
TRACY Washington.

> *The* UNPLEASANT MAN *has been corrected in public. He's angry. The air is now charged.*

LITTLE OLD LADY Excuse me, sir, but smoking is a danger to health and a hazard to life and is not permitted on the underground.

> *Again he glares and then ignores her.*

Well you can glare all you like, sir, but experience has taught us a lesson and I'm going to keep on asking you – please put out your cigarette. There are other people in this carriage who have to be considered. [*No response*] I mean you don't live on this earth by yourself, sir. Someone's driving this train for you and someone made your jacket for you and I assume you had a good breakfast this morning. [*No response*] Can you hear me? [*No response*] Are you listening, sir?
SAM Why's she keep calling him 'sir'?
LITTLE OLD LADY Do you enjoy upsetting other people?

> *He opens his newspaper as though to escape her.*

People like him make it a really depressing day. Just

takes one person and you feel all human nature is rotten.

> *Silence.*

I suppose he's imagining he's exercising his democratic rights.

> *No comment.*

Well let me tell you, sir, if you'll forgive me lecturing you, sir, and I know I'm only a foolish old woman with everything finished and failed behind me, and you're a splendid young man with everything brave and shining ahead of him, let me tell you — democratic rights have their limitations. They have! *Your* democratic rights are limited by *our* democratic rights. And it's our democratic right not to have to breathe in the foul smoke of your cigarette or run the risk of going up in flames. What do you say to that?

SAM Subtle!

> *The* UNPLEASANT MAN *turns a fierce gaze upon* SAM.

It's the capital of Madagascar. [*Points to book*] Subtle — capital of Madagascar.

UNPLEASANT MAN I know what 'subtle' means, sonny. I'm not stupid. Play your games and mind your own business.

LITTLE OLD LADY It is his business. His life's under threat because of you.

UNPLEASANT MAN And you think yourself lucky you're an old woman.

LITTLE OLD LADY No, you think yourself lucky I'm an old woman, and this is a poor mother, and these are only young children and that there's no one here to yank that weed from your mouth and stand ten feet taller than you.

UNPLEASANT MAN You can yank it out, lady. Be my guest. Anyone can be my guest.

> *No one takes up his invitation.*
>
> *The train stops. Sound of doors opening.*
>
> JASON *gets on. He has a Walkman plugged into his ears and is dancing to himself to music that cannot be heard other than the maddening bass beat of 'dud, dud, dud'.*
>
> *Sound of doors closing. Train moves off.*
>
> JASON *is oblivious to the tension. Dances on. All regard him except the* UNPLEASANT MAN *and the* LITTLE OLD LADY *who is watching the* UNPLEASANT MAN.
>
> *Suddenly* JASON *notices and slowly comes to a halt.*

JASON [*To* HARASSED WOMAN] Hey, man. He's smoking.

TRACY   [*Together*]   You could've fooled me.
SAM   Nah! You're imagining it.

> *The* UNPLEASANT MAN *turns his fierce gaze first upon* SAM *and* TRACY *who huddle down, then upon* JASON *who, frightened, returns to his jigging.*

JASON Cool, man, cool! It's a free country. Cool.

LITTLE OLD LADY Free for you, too, young man.

JASON Yes, ma'am, I know that. Look [*dancing*] *I'm* free!

LITTLE OLD LADY Chained to one of those things? [*No response*] While you're dancing Rome may burn.

JASON [*To* SAM *and* TRACY] She do exaggerate don't she!

LITTLE OLD LADY And you're the only one here who's his size.

JASON Please, ma'am. My life gives me enough headaches. My brother's in jail, my girl's left me, I don't like my job and my motor bike's been nicked. I can only take on board so much or I'll sink. This gentleman here may be my size but he's not my type. My type is reasonable, co-operative, full of love and tenderness with two kind eyes in a friendly head. Know what I mean? You seen that man's eyes? Them's the unhappiest eyes I've seen in a long time. He don't like himself one little bit. That man's got an inferiority complex the size of a volcano and there ain't nothing more unpredictable and dangerous than a volcano, ma'am, I'm telling you. Now, do you mind, excuse me, I've got to get back to my therapy.

> *He returns to his dancing. The joy is gone, though. He's more apprehensive.*

LITTLE OLD LADY Is no one going to stand up to this oaf?

> *The* UNPLEASANT MAN *steps towards her, threateningly.*

[*Defiantly*] Hit me!

> *He considers it. All watch. Thinks better of it.*
> *Grins. Returns to his newspaper.*

TRACY Capital of India?
SAM Dunno.
TRACY Delhi. Capital of Canada?
SAM Dunno.
TRACY Montreal. Capital of Ireland?
SAM [*Surprised at himself*] Dublin!
UNPLEASANT MAN Thank bloody Christ!

> *Train stops. Sound of doors opening.*
>
> *His cigarette is at an end. He stubs it out with*
> *his foot.*
>
> *Sound of doors closing. Train moves off.*
>
> *Tension eases. A kind of normality returns.*
>
> *Only the sound of the train and the 'dud, dud,*
> *dud' from the Walkman.*
>
> *Very slowly and deliberately the* UNPLEASANT
> MAN *takes out his packet of cigarettes and*
> *places one in his mouth.*
>
> *Everyone turns to see what he'll do. Even*
> JASON *ceases moving.*
>
> *The tension has risen again.*
>
> *He takes out a lighter. Before he can strike it*
> *the* LITTLE OLD LADY *stands up.*

LITTLE OLD LADY You light that cigarette and I'll pull
this chain.

> *She raises her hand to the Emergency chain.*
> *Confrontation.*
>
> *The* UNPLEASANT MAN *is held. He's having*
> *second thoughts. His face is full of fury.*
>
> *The tension is unbearable.*

JASON Oh, ma'am, give us a break, ma'am. You pull
that chain and the train will stop and then all the
other trains will have to stop and maybe something
will go wrong and there'll be a crash and people will
die or get hurt just for one man who so badly needs a
drag he can't hold back.

LITTLE OLD LADY I smoke thirty a day. I can hold back.

JASON You're stronger than he is. Anyone can see that.

LITTLE OLD LADY [*To* UNPLEASANT MAN] Light it and
I'll pull.

> *The tension is now so unbearable that the*
> HARASSED WOMAN *bursts out.*

HARASSED WOMAN You pull that chain and I'll be late
for my appointment. One late appointment leads to
another. And there's someone looking after my
children who has their own appointments. Why are
you making trouble? What's in a cigarette? One
cigarette in a whole carriage. No one else is smoking
and no one else is complaining. Can you see anyone
else smoking? Can you hear anyone else
complaining? You frightened from the smoke of one
cigarette? Open the windows. Look! I'll open them.
This one, and this one, and this one. There! There
won't be any smoke now and all of us can detect
smouldering in time – only don't pull that chain or

you'll upset everyone's life. For one man! One anti-social man and a lousy cigarette.

> *Silence.*
> *Only the train and the 'dud, dud, dud'.*
> *What will he do? What will she do?*

LITTLE OLD LADY Light it. I pull.

> *The question and answer between* SAM *and* TRACY *continues, but really their concentration is on the* UNPLEASANT MAN.

TRACY Capital of Denmark?
SAM Dunno.
TRACY Copenhagen. Capital of Zimbabwe?
SAM Dunno.
TRACY Harare. Capital of Israel?
SAM [*Hopefully*] Jerusalem?

> *He lights. She pulls.*
> *Blackout*
> *Sound of train, now loud, screeches to a halt.*
> *A babble of complaining voices.*
> *Cut out.*
> *Silence.*
> *End.*

THE GREAT CAMEL RUMBLES AND GROANS AND SPITS

HENRY LIVINGS

Characters

DRUMMER	
HEAD MAN	
KILAK	a young bride from a far country
LUO	her husband
ANANSI	who appears to be a scrawny old lady, but will reveal a secret during the play (this one should be played by a boy)
GREAT CAMEL	
CAMEL TOO	
Womenfolk:	BISO, CHIQUI, NAHKI, AND SOPI
Menfolk:	LABONGO AND KIPIR

The setting is a hot place, where, with some travelling, you could reach the desert: Africa, Asia, Australia, or Central America. If you choose one of these in particular, and research it, there'll be a consistency about such things as masks, the drum, etc. If the audience can see the stage floor, it could be painted, say green and brown strips, so that the people can step over green and hoe brown as if in the field. The trick with the hoe is to sneak another shorter one on each time, so it's probably better to have some place of concealment, say a screen, though any magician will tell you that if you have some noticeable action on one side, the audience doesn't see what's happening the other side.

Masks, ceremonial, hardly at all naturalistic; they represent spirits, like the heraldic devices of Europe.

Clothes, say a simple shift; this is an egalitarian society, flip-flops maybe. Camels, if you go and look, are loosely assembled, and their feet don't go down in a neat orderly way; ours is one person behind another, the same simple clothes as the rest, with a fringed umbrella to represent the hump. When the umbrella is folded, and the mask doffed, the camel disappears, right? Make sure the mouth of the camel's mask is clear . . . camels are noisy articles; some masks have a built-in megaphone.

The trick with the arms near the end, if you want to do it, is to use one off a tailor's dummy (darken the knuckles a bit, they look unconvincingly clean), hidden inside the actor's shift until required.
Watch out there are no electric sockets where the 'irrigation' piddle can reach.

Plays are of course games, and therefore serious. This one is about how a stranger is received and how she keeps the soul of her own people with her in a strange land. In the African original, it's an ox, not a camel, and it dies at the end; when she reports this to her own people, they all cut their throats, because without their spirit, they will go mad. By having a camel instead, we get more fun, but also camel says 'desert', doesn't it? And I think we'd find it hard to take him dying; to a peasant African, the death of a spirit isn't a permanent one, the spirit of the lion lives on in all lions even when one is hunted and killed, as Christians believe Jesus lives. An itinerant story-teller in Africa is telling the story to villagers who manifestly still have their particular spirit (they're still alive), so his story must be about some other people; if we all started cutting our throats in the school assembly, our audience would think we were weird.

DRUMMER This is a story of the high and far off time, before the Mox.
This drum is for calling a Council, but the people are all long dead. This drum calls ghosts, they know the words it speaks.

[*He drums*] 'Let the Nation come to the Council.'

> *And the company start to arrive, one step at a time, like the game of statues; there's the* HEAD MAN *with his ceremonial walking-stick,* KILAK, LUO, ANANSI, *the* WOMENFOLK *and the* MENFOLK. *They form a circle . . only in the centre space may anyone speak publicly. The* HEAD MAN *takes the centre to open the Council formally.*

HEAD MAN Luo, why is this Council called? [*He immediately retires, as will all the others, once they've had their say.*]
KILAK It's not fair!
DRUMMER Be quiet Kilak, the Head Man speaks first, women last.

LUO I asked for the Council to be called sir; there has been no Dance of Welcome for Kilak my bride; none of the other women help her in the field; this isn't how neighbours should be, especially to a stranger.

HEAD MAN What do the women say?

BOSI We treat her as fairly as we can, but she doesn't help herself!

CHIQUI Luo took nine cows out of the village as a bride price to Kilak's father; those cows will never be ours again.

NAHKI He brings a stranger here, who doesn't know the customs, who can't tend his field, and expects us to help her!

SOPI Her family is a month's travel away, what happens when she's in childbirth?

KILAK It's not fair!

DRUMMER If you can't keep your woman quiet Luo, someone will have to do it for you.

HEAD MAN She doesn't know the customs, let her learn them. Women, please do the Hoe Dance.

> *The* WOMEN *don their masks, take up hoes, the* DRUMMER *drums for them, and they dance a simple measure, stabbing down efficiently with the hoes, screwing out the weeds to be trampled, heaping the soil back round the roots;* KILAK, *who has no mask, struggles to imitate their skill, sweating and watching the others intently. After one figure, she is weary of the sun and the work, lays aside the hoe, and bends, hands pressed on her knees, to ease her back. The drum continues, as the others huddle in a scrum against her, sneaking her hoe in among them; the sound of sawing and a*

*bustle in the bunch as two hold and one saws.
The* MEN *crane noisily to see what's to do.
Then the hoe is replaced and the dance
resumed as before. Refreshed,* KILAK *grabs the
hoe, and tries again. Only this time the hoe is
some six inches shorter, and she is all the
sooner tired.
The scrum, the sawing noise, the bustle, the
craning men beginning to smirk in
comprehension, and the hoe replaced again.
This time it's another foot shorter, and she's
rapidly crippled with backache and on her
knees, desperately trying to keep up.*

KILAK It's not fair! Luo!

*But he's too embarrassed to help her in front
of others. The Dance concludes; they reform
the circle, take off their masks.* KILAK *centre,
kneeling, head bowed.*

HEAD MAN Kilak, your hoe is too short, can't you tell?
KILAK How do I know? I've never even seen a hoe
before I came here! I don't know what they're
supposed to be like.

*Stunned pause, everybody crowding to look at
this oddity.*

HEAD MAN Luo, either your bride is a liar, or she's a
fool, or she's lazy beyond the power of man to
describe.

ANANSI [*Gabble gabble*] She's all three! All three! All
  three!

KILAK If you want me to milk a goat, dress and cook a
  ewe lamb for a feast, spin and weave, I can do it.
  Teach me to hoe and I'll hoe!

DRUMMER Don't talk back to the Head Man Kilak!
  Speak civilly, show respect.

ANANSI She's all three! All three! All three!

KILAK You tell me to be quiet, and you let a batty old
  woman go gabbling on like a throttling hen bird.

HEAD MAN That is enough! Anansi is a woman far
  gone in years, for that she must be respected: her
  experience is our book. Anansi, have you ever
  known such a thing before? A woman who neglects
  her husband's fields? What was done in past times?
  What's your opinion?

ANANSI *has a good think. Goes to the centre.*
Thinks again. Gazes up.

ANANSI I'm hungry!

HEAD MAN Anansi, you always talk sense; it'll be dark
  soon, time we all ate. Council is over.

DRUMMER Council is over!

As the others drift away, LUO *squats facing*
KILAK.

LUO Woman what are we going to do?

She shrugs, dispirited.

LUO There's only one little pot of cornmeal that I
brought from my mother's house, and two quail that
I shot today. After what's just happened, my mother
will be ashamed, she won't want to feed you.

KILAK My people would share, they'd be ashamed not
to.

LUO So would we, but after that Council? What
compound can we walk in to where they wouldn't
snigger to our faces?

KILAK Is that what I get for a month's hard walking?

LUO Corn takes half a year to grow; my field is stiff
with weeds, dry as snuff, we shall be begging for
food.

KILAK I'm a bad wife; they all despise me. D'you
despise me?

LUO [*Puts his hand on her shoulder*] I'll give my
mother the quail; she'll put vegetables to them and
cook them. She'll want me to try some, I'll praise her
cooking, tell her how delicious it is, say I have to be
going, that you'll have my meal ready, and she'll give
me some to bring away with me.

> *For a moment they look at each other, trying*
> *to muster a smile between them.*

KILAK I was so happy, coming to a new life with you,
in a far off place, the walk wasn't hard.

> LUO *bows his head and goes.*
>
> KILAK *presses her hands to her face to keep out*
> *the light, curls up on the floor, and sleeps,*
> *alone.*
>
> *After a still moment, a great rumbling*
> *Harrrumph echoes out.*

> KILAK *sleeps on.*
>
> *And the* GREAT CAMEL, *closely followed by*
> CAMEL TOO, *who carries a fringed umbrella*
> *and a dung bucket, enters, shambling untidily*
> *to* KILAK, *rumbling and groaning and spitting*
> *like a vast stomach-ache.*

GREAT CAMEL Harrrrumph.

KILAK [*Quite still, opens her eyes*] Who are you?

GREAT CAMEL I am the Great Camel.

CAMEL TOO And I'm Camel Too.

CAMEL I come from the high and far off time. Before
the Mox.

> CAMEL TOO *bows slowly till his head is*
> *between his knees, still holding the umbrella*
> *up, and blows a rasping juicy raspberry. The*
> GREAT CAMEL *swivels his mournful haughty*
> *head to regard this disrespectful mutineer, and*
> *back to look at* KILAK.

KILAK Where am I?

GREAT CAMEL Your husband's field.

> *The* GREAT CAMEL *and* CAMEL TOO *begin to*
> *sway and shamble, one behind the other, back*
> *and forth, scuffling their feet to scuff up weeds*
> *and trample them and to shore up earth round*
> *the roots, along the furrows.*

KILAK [*Sits up*] Is this a dream?

GREAT CAMEL No.

> ANANSI *creeps on in the background, a half-*
> *eaten corncob in her hand, senile, nosy and*
> *gleeful. She cups her hand to her ear, but it's*
> *doubtful she can hear a lot, she strains too*
> *much.* CAMEL TOO *drops two dollops of dung*
> *as they go.*

KILAK What are you doing?

CAMEL TOO Dunging the earth.

KILAK Oh, mucky sod, and I've got to work here you
know, all day.

GREAT CAMEL Dunging enriches the earth.

KILAK I bet it does. I think it *is* a dream.

> *Up and down they go, swinging their legs and*
> *feet any old which way, scuffle, scuffle.*

GREAT CAMEL Once, in your country, where there is
now fine brown dust, there was dark moist earth;
where there is scrub and parched grass rattles in the
wind, there were shaded green orange groves, pale
olives, lemons like lanterns weighing down the
branches to the ground.

> *They pause;* CAMEL TOO *straddles, leaning on*
> GREAT CAMEL, *takes a small watering-can from*
> *the bucket, and pours a splat or two on to the*
> *earth, then they shamble on.*

Your people dug long straight irrigation channels,
and cold clear water ran day and night; there were
fish, and broad reeds for basket-making.

KILAK In my country?
GREAT CAMEL Harrrumph.
KILAK Will my husband's field be like that?
GREAT CAMEL Harrrrrumph!

> ANANSI *lets a long breath of amazement
> out* WHEEEEE!, *and tosses her corncob in the
> air, moves to catch it, realises she's revealed
> herself, and looks to the others just in time for
> the corncob to descend bonk on her nut. She's
> even more amazed to see no* CAMEL, *but two*
> YOUNG MEN, *one with a basket, (the camel-
> mask held by the strap) and the other with a
> folded umbrella and a bucket.*

ANANSI She's all three! All three! All three!

> BOSI *enters, stops at the sight of two strangers.*

BOSI [*To* ANANSI, *referring to* KILAK] It's decided to get
up in a morning, has it?

> *The* GREAT CAMEL *gives a great rumble,
> harrumph, and a spit.* ANANSI *and* BOSI *spin to
> see who did it.* CHIQUI *arrives for work.*

CHIQUI What's going on?
BOSI Kilak's husband's field, look, all the weeds hoe'd
out, the soil neat round the planting, and *watered*.
And it's only just daybreak.

> *A high tight raspberry from* CAMEL TOO, *a haughty stare of reproof from the* GREAT CAMEL.*
>
> *The* WOMEN'S *eyes move from* KILAK *to the* GREAT CAMEL *and back.*

ANANSI She's all three!

> NAHKI *and* SOPI *arrive for work.*
>
> *Gasping,* ANANSI *gets them all into a huddle to tell about the strange beast, her bony arm flailing as she describes the size, the weird shape, the head.*
>
> *The* DRUMMER *crosses, notices the two balls of dung, stops, sniffs, looks about: what kind of beast left that? Sees* CAMEL TOO *and the* GREAT CAMEL.*

DRUMMER Erm, good day strangers . . .

> *The* GREAT CAMEL *and* CAMEL TOO *gravely incline their heads.*

NAHKI Drummer, you must call a Council!

DRUMMER [*After a glance towards the womenfolk, turns back*] I can't make out what could have left that, I cannot. Did you see an unusually large beast?

CHIQUI Are you listening?

DRUMMER It's not elephant, it's too big for elephant. What?

SOPI Call a Council!

DRUMMER Eh? You can't ask for a Council to be called, it's against custom. [*To* CAMEL TOO] I see you have an umbrella sir, would you be the Head Man where you come from?

> CAMEL TOO *shakes his head, indicates the* GREAT CAMEL.

DRUMMER Ah. Excuse me sir, the women here, they're getting above themselves, I shall have to deal with them.

ANANSI She's all three!

DRUMMER [*After a careful weigh-up*] Sometimes your words are too wise for me Anansi. [*To them all*] What's this Council for did you say?

BOSI Call the Council, then you'll find out what it's for.

DRUMMER You know the custom: the Head Man must be told, and he tells me, and I call the Council; it's men's work; the Head Man would think we were trying to get rid of him.

CHIQUI Look at Kilak's field.

> He looks round, inspects, carefully keeping to the furrows.

KILAK Oh, so it's Kilak's field now is it? What happened to Kilak's husband's field?

> Hostile stares. The DRUMMER returns to the group, awestruck.

DRUMMER What happened to Kilak's husband's field?

NAHKI Call a Council, then you'll find out.

ANANSI Huge, with a head like two heads one above the other! A back like two backs one above the other!

> *The* DRUMMER *drums, feverish. The company form the Council circle, one step at a time. The* HEAD MAN *goes to centre, raises his hand for the drum to stop.*

HEAD MAN Why is this Council called? [*He looks from dumb face to dumb face. He tries the drummer.*] Who's the strangers?

DRUMMER [*Sotto*] Seem to be dumb, or don't speak our language; the one without the umbrella is some sort of Head Man where they come from.

HEAD MAN [*Elaborate, as to a deaf idiot*] Well-come sir! I Am Thee Head Man Here! At least I think I am. I still have my ceremonial walking-stick. Yes. [*Backs off, smirking sweatily; grips the* DRUMMER] This is completely against custom; why the Council drumtalk? Why wasn't I told about important visitors?

KILAK I see a man who invents places for other people to be in.

> *The* DRUMMER *and the* HEAD MAN *have a good look at this weirdo.*

DRUMMER It was the womenfolk.

HEAD MAN Am I Head Man here or not? Just let me know! The womenfolk! Women don't call the Council; it's men's work! Why?

DRUMMER Exactly.

HEAD MAN Exactly what?

> *The* DRUMMER *in mental agony what to say,*
> *writhes about for an excuse.*

LABONGO He's losing his touch, our Head Man is.

KIPIR The Drummer doesn't look in very good order
either. Well, there's others I daresay. [*He means the*
GREAT CAMEL]

LABONGO [*Has a look*] Cool hm?

KILAK [*In wonderment*] My spirit is here, now; the
Great Camel.

HEAD MAN What? What's going on? People are
muttering.

DRUMMER Eeeeeagh . . . eeagh!

HEAD MAN [*Stopped*] What is it? Stomach-ache?

DRUMMER Head-ache.

HEAD MAN This is hardly the time; get yourself to
Anansi, she has all the wisdom of our nation, from
the high and far off time, before the Mox. She'll put
you right.

> [ANANSI *comes to centre, gazes vaguely about.*   ]

KIPIR [*He means the* HEAD MAN] He's floundering isn't
he?

LABONGO Anansi's working him from behind; he
daren't piss without asking her first. Look at the
stranger, he's got some dignity and authority about
him eh?

KIPIR [*Nodding agreement*] Never opens his muff.

ANANSI Huge! With a head like two heads one above
the other, a back like two backs one above the other!

DRUMMER That's it! That's it exactly: a Great Beast, in
the night, probably trampling every field, [*Hastily,
since it isn't trampled here* . . .] except Kilak's.
Huge, bigger than an elephant. [*Points dramatically
at the dung* . . .] There's its dung!

HEAD MAN [*Starts back, inspects; makes up his manly mind*] Men! Fetch spears! Fetch your bows! We may need nets too! Women! Start the Hunting Dance please!

BOSI Our fields aren't trampled, are they?

KILAK I see a man in trouble with himself who tells us we're all in trouble. I see a man who starts on killing when his dignity and authority are threatened.

HEAD MAN [*An uneasy look round for this man or men*] What? You be careful what you say young woman, that's witch's talk.

> *The* DRUMMER *drums* 'The Nation gathers for the Hunt'. *The* WOMENFOLK *form a straight line, as for beating game out of cover, put on masks.*

HEAD MAN [*Shoves her in line*] Kilak, learn our customs; the Great Beast must be hunted and killed before it brings us to starvation and death.

KILAK Why? What's it ever done?

> *The* MENFOLK *are returned with their weapons; they wear masks, and bring masks for the* GREAT CAMEL *and* CAMEL TOO, *honoured guests.*

LUO [*Whips off his mask to rebuke his wife*] Woman!

KILAK Please! Luo, why?

LUO [*Grips her*] Learn the customs. [*Gives her her mask.*]

> *The* DANCE *is a simple set of crouching paces for the* MEN, *with emphasis on the forward step, the spear or bow slashed rhythmically as*

if hacking through bush, and then raised and thrust AH! AH! AH!, *and for the* WOMEN *a neat small round-step, hands clapping above the head, and a shrill* LILILILIL . . . *to scare the quarry into the open, and then as the* MEN *thrust, a swooping swivel as if lifting the dead animal high in triumph. The Dance concludes, all leave.*

Then KILAK *runs back, fearful of discovery, takes off her mask, puts her head in her hands to hold the grief for her friend. Finally . . .*

KILAK It's not fair.

A silence. Then, very faint and distant, but growing through the next scene, the tap-tap-tap of the drum 'the hunt comes home, the hunt has been successful . . .'

ANANSI *creeps on, squats by* KILAK, *not looking at her; scratches the ground with a stick, wonders what the sign is she's scratched; takes out her corncob, nibbles a bit. Glances sideways at* KILAK, *and away.*

ANANSI [*Quietly*] Are you a witch?

KILAK [*After a moment*] No.

ANANSI The women think you're a witch already, so it doesn't make any difference does it?

KILAK What will they do?

ANANSI [*Has another nibble*] Shun you. A witch's secret sight makes them uneasy.

KILAK They shun me already, so it doesn't make any difference does it?

ANANSI [*Titters absently*] Are you a witch? [*No answer*] I'm a witch too; my spirit was in a monkey. He died.

KILAK That's daft.

ANANSI Yes. [*A sideways look, then*] Your spirit was in the Great Camel wasn't it?

KILAK *stares at her: how did she know that?*

ANANSI I told you, I'm a witch.

KILAK It's as if you hear my thoughts clearer than my spoken words.

ANANSI I'm a witch, did I tell you, and I'm a spider. [*Out from her shift, there appears another arm, which she raises before* KILAK'S *forehead in blessing, then offers the hand of friendship*] I've got another as well, six limbs altogether, I told you. I'm a mystery to myself. I'm a man, and a spider, and my experience is the nation's book.

The drum is nearly upon us.

KILAK The Head Man says you're a woman.

ANANSI What does he know when I don't know myself? I'm all three!

The COMPANY, *led by* LUO *carrying the* GREAT CAMEL'S *mask, process at a slow dance, across and away; the* WOMEN *carry* GREAT CAMEL *and* CAMEL TOO *on poles, the heads of the victims wrapped in rough hoods of ragged scarlet cloth.* ANANSI *joins on the end, gleeful and prancing, back to two arms now.* LUO *waits for a word with* KILAK *as the others leave.*

ANANSI In three days, a feast! a feast! a feast!

LUO [*Kneels, offers the mask*] Kilak, I spoke harshly to you before; it hurt my heart then, and it hurts it now.

> *She shakes her head sadly, it doesn't matter; avoids looking at the mask.*

LUO I've brought you home the mask; it's my trophy, I was the first to strike.

> *She nods her dumb head up and down.*

LUO The people want you to cook the feast; they'll bring vegetables; they'll joint the carcass. They honour you.

KILAK They don't honour me; they think I'm a witch; they want to see me cook my own spirit.

LUO [*After a pause, he knows she's right*] Will you do it? Please. Prove you're just like them.

> *Slowly, she nods her dumb head.* LUO *goes, leaving the mask.*

KILAK [*When he's gone*] Prove I'm just like them. Hah!

> *The* MEN, *in their masks, bring two large cooking-pots;* BOSI *brings a bowl of (pre-cooked) vegetables; they sit, immobile, to watch* KILAK *cook; the rest of the* COMPANY *join them, a silent, still witness. The* DRUMMER *and*

the HEAD MAN, *not masked, to either side. The* HEAD MAN *hands her a knife, ceremonially. As she cuts up and adds the vegetables, a smell of cooking onions, veg, lentils and spice wafts among us. Meanwhile, the* DRUMMER *taps out, light and merry . . .*

'Feast time is here, everybody come and eat, feast time . . .'

ANANSI, *unmasked, crouches like a heap of rags in the* COMPANY.

DRUMMER [*As he drums*] One night, one day,
⠀⠀⠀⠀⠀⠀⠀⠀⠀⠀⠀⠀⠀⠀⠀One night, one day,
⠀⠀⠀⠀⠀⠀⠀⠀⠀⠀⠀⠀⠀⠀⠀One night, the ghosts
⠀⠀⠀⠀⠀⠀⠀⠀⠀⠀⠀⠀⠀⠀⠀Of the people, watched.
⠀⠀⠀⠀⠀⠀⠀⠀⠀⠀⠀⠀⠀⠀⠀And Kilak prepared
⠀⠀⠀⠀⠀⠀⠀⠀⠀⠀⠀⠀⠀⠀⠀The feast of her life.
⠀⠀⠀⠀⠀⠀⠀⠀⠀⠀⠀⠀⠀⠀⠀They slept with their eyes open
⠀⠀⠀⠀⠀⠀⠀⠀⠀⠀⠀⠀⠀⠀⠀They would not miss a second
⠀⠀⠀⠀⠀⠀⠀⠀⠀⠀⠀⠀⠀⠀⠀Of her pain, but they slept . . .

KILAK *takes the* GREAT CAMEL'S *mask, and kneels by the vegetable bowl, in front of the cooking-pots. Takes fronds of herbs, and lays them on the mask. Bows to rest her forehead against the* GREAT CAMEL'S . . .

⠀⠀⠀⠀⠀⠀⠀⠀⠀⠀⠀⠀⠀⠀⠀And as the smoke
⠀⠀⠀⠀⠀⠀⠀⠀⠀⠀⠀⠀⠀⠀⠀Of her life, rose
⠀⠀⠀⠀⠀⠀⠀⠀⠀⠀⠀⠀⠀⠀⠀Above the fires
⠀⠀⠀⠀⠀⠀⠀⠀⠀⠀⠀⠀⠀⠀⠀She cherished with herbs
⠀⠀⠀⠀⠀⠀⠀⠀⠀⠀⠀⠀⠀⠀⠀The strange head.
⠀⠀⠀⠀⠀⠀⠀⠀⠀⠀⠀⠀⠀⠀⠀And at a time in the night
⠀⠀⠀⠀⠀⠀⠀⠀⠀⠀⠀⠀⠀⠀⠀Which nobody knew
⠀⠀⠀⠀⠀⠀⠀⠀⠀⠀⠀⠀⠀⠀⠀Or will ever . . .

*He stops drumming in mid-beat. All still, eyes
open, as the Voice of the* GREAT CAMEL
*harrrumphs, groans, and grumbles, and spits.
Then the* GREAT CAMEL, *and* CAMEL TOO, *take
off their Hunter masks, rise, and wobble
ungainly forward, rumbling, groaning and
spitting, pick up the umbrella, and the bucket.*
CAMEL TOO *helps the* GREAT CAMEL *to reattach
one of his arms.*
KILAK *rises like a sleep-walker, holding up the
mask, the face towards hers.
The* GREAT CAMEL, *gangling and clumsy,
nuzzles his head into the mask.*
CAMEL TOO *just about makes it to his place
behind the* GREAT CAMEL, *leans on him to be
able to get his head between his knees, and
then gives a fine gigantic raspberry.
The disdainful head swivels to regard this
vulgarian, and then lifts to give a great rutting
roar like a stag with asthma. Then he lays his
head on* KILAK'S *shoulder for a moment, and
they shamble off, rumble grumble groan spit.*

DRUMMER . . . or will ever know. Before the Mox.
[*And he drums again as if nothing had intervened
as* . . .]

The COMPANY *gather, dancing as they wait in a
queue, and paper plates are brought, and they
and we partake of spicy vegetable stew. But
first, the* HEAD MAN *tastes* . . .

HEAD MAN Kilak, either you're a very good cook, or a
very wise woman to invoke the spirits over your
work, or you're a witch!

ANANSI [*Food all over the place, and her*] She's all
three! All three! All three!

A SLIGHT HITCH
JULIET ACE

Characters

JOSIE

LINDY

GINA

CLEANER

'RUNAWAY GIRLS LIVE ON MOTORWAY.' This newspaper headline nagged at me for days until I was compelled to write *A Slight Hitch*.

Is life so unbearable for some young girls that they leave home in desperation? Do they leave in the hope that someone will run after them and beg them to return home? Is it a cry for help? Do they imagine that life anywhere but home must be better?

And when they've plucked up the courage to go, what then?

> *The lights come up on the ladies cloakroom of a motorway transport café. It is a tiled room with two lavatories. There are washbasins with mirrors above, soap containers, a powerful hand-dryer and a chair.*
>
> JOSIE, *an Afro-Caribbean Brummie, is in one of the lavatories, singing. She breaks into a rap of her own making.*

JOSIE [*Improvising*] I walked outa my house . . . I
   didn't look back . . . No, I didn't look back. No
   Sir . . . I'm beatin' a track and I won't look back . . .
   on my Mum and the kids, and the beatins and the
   shoutin . . . [*She hums*]

> LINDY, *a Londoner, comes into the cloakroom.*
> *She's beginning to get the shakes. Her face is*
> *very white, her eyes dark and dead. She sits on*
> *the chair and fumbles in her bag for a syringe.*
> JOSIE *stops singing.*

JOSIE [*In lavatory*] Hello? . . . Who's that?
LINDY Lindy.
JOSIE Hi. You all right?
LINDY Yeah.

> JOSIE *flushes the lavatory and comes out. She*
> *has a scruffy holdall.*

JOSIE You all right?
LINDY Yeah.

> LINDY *gets up and staggers into a lavatory.*

LINDY Watch my things.
JOSIE Sure.

> JOSIE *looks in the mirror. She examines her*
> *face carefully.*

JOSIE Time for a good wash. He's got apple pie, tea
   and a fag to get through yet . . . There's no telling
   when we'll get another chance. Jason's great isn't

he? He's really stuck on us . . . [*She sniffs her
armpits*] Phew. I niff a bit . . . the cab in that lorry
gets really hot, yeh? Forgot to spray myself this
morning. Hey, d'you think they'll scream if I take
my blouse off and wash the sleeve bits? Lindy?
LINDY What?
JOSIE There was this girl I knew at school . . . She went
on the road for a bit. [*She takes her blouse off*]
Came home to have a kid. She said to look òut for
toilets with blow hand-dryers . . . handy if there's
time to spare [*She giggles*] Miniature laundrette this.
Liquid soap.

> *She rubs it into the underarms of her blouse,
> being careful not to wet the rest of it. She rinses
> it under the tap.*

LINDY [*Between her teeth*] Oh God . . . Oh God . . .
Oh God . . .
JOSIE Lindy . . . Are you OK? Lindy?
LINDY Mmm.
JOSIE Right.

> JOSIE *pulls out a paper towel from a dispenser
> and squeezes it into the blouse.*

JOSIE This'll absorb most of the wet. OK. Now for the
dryer.

> JOSIE *holds the blouse over the dryer, so that
> the hot air blows down one sleeve. The
> billowing blouse amuses her. Then she gets
> bored.*

I can't stand here holding it all the time.

> *She tries to fix it unsuccessfully to the dryer.*
> *She thinks hard.*

I know. Chewing-gum.

LINDY What are you doing now? You stupid cow.

> JOSIE *gets some chewing-gum from her bag and*
> *chews and bubbles it at a terrific rate. When it*
> *is stretchy, she sticks her blouse to the dryer*
> *with it.*

JOSIE Good. Chewing-gum cleans your teeth as well. I forgot to pack a toothbrush. Anyway me and the kids use the same one.

LINDY You don't share toothbrushes. You don't share syringes. You don't share apples . . . Don't you read the newspaper . . .?

JOSIE Never.

LINDY Or watch the telly?

> JOSIE *breathes on her hand.*

JOSIE I wish I could tell if I've got bad breath.

> JOSIE *starts the process of washing, beginning*
> *with her face.*

How long is it since I met you, Lindy . . . two days? No not quite. Dinner-time, yesterday. I feel as if I've known you forever. Don't know anyone back home.

The kids at school are all jerks. I'm never there. Too much to do. God, my Mum's a slag. A real slag. It's me looks after the kids. Even little Jamie. He thinks I'm his mother. Right, I said. I'm getting out. So I left.

> GINA *comes into the cloakroom.* GINA *has been on the road a long time and knows the ropes. She's sixteen but looks twenty five. Her bare legs are artificially tanned and look good with her stiletto-heeled shoes. She starts to brush her hair and touch up her make-up. She looks at* JOSIE *in the mirror.*

JOSIE What are you looking at?

GINA You. It's a free country.

LINDY Watch my bag.

JOSIE Don't worry I am.

GINA [*Mimicking*] Watch my bag. I don't suppose you've got anything worth nicking.

JOSIE Stop staring, right.

GINA I should go home love.

JOSIE Oh yeh.

GINA New to the game, aren't you? I should go home. Stick to somewhere you know.

JOSIE Hear that, Lindy?

GINA [*Spraying perfume behind her ears*] You've got to know what you're doing.

JOSIE And you do?

GINA I can look after myself. You? You're a baby. There's a lot of weirdos out there. You've got to know what's what.

> GINA *bangs the lavatory door.*

Isn't that right, Lindy? Just 'cos a fella's got a pretty face doesn't mean he's straight. What's she doing in there?

JOSIE Mind your own business.

GINA Oh yes. [*To Lindy*] You want to kick that little lot and all, love. It's a mug's game.

> *She closes her bag. She whispers to* JOSIE.

Drop her.

> GINA *leaves.*

JOSIE Bloody nerve. I don't need anyone telling me what to do. Right, Lindy?

LINDY Right.

> JOSIE *fixes the other arm of the blouse to the dryer. She washes under her arms.*

JOSIE When I get settled, I'm going to have a little room and do it up. Get a proper job . . . in a shop, p'raps, for starters. Fancy being nearly back in Brum. Yesterday morning when I got my first lift out . . . I thought . . . a couple of hours and I'll be in London. It's that bloody Jason's fault. Two hours in London and here we are in bloody Brum again. Still it's worth it. Jason's fantastic. Not like the kids at

home. He's brilliant. And then we picked you up. I
don't mind Lindy . . . the three of us. It'll be great.
Stick together, right. See the world. My blouse is
nearly dry.

> *She looks at her feet.*

God, look at my feet. God they're stinking. I'll do
them too.

> *She sits on a chair and takes her sandals off.*

I've got good feet. They measure your feet down the
Sosh. Weird shoes . . . good fit.

> *She puts two paper towels on the floor. She
> fills a basin with water and washes one foot,
> then the other.*

Yeh. All our kids have got good feet. God . . . I bet
Jamie's missing me. Missing me like hell. I wonder
who picked him up from the minder. Not 'er.

> *She remembers a bruise on her thigh.*

God this bruise has really come out now. All
swollen. Bloody old slag. 'That's the last time you hit
me,' I said to her. It made me scream . . . the pain.
She went for our Precious 'cos she'd peed in her bed
again . . . She can't help it. If she didn't stay out half
the night she could pot her. I pulled Precious away

from her, then I swore at her. Cow. 'My kids
don't bloody swear at me.' I just laughed. So she got
me with the bread-board. That did it. Do you know
what Jason said to me last night? He said I could be
a model.

> LINDY *comes out at last. She's back to her*
> *bright self again.*

LINDY You don't 'alf rabbit on.
JOSIE Sorry. You could be a model . . . with that hair.
   Those legs.

> LINDY *splashes cold water onto her face.*

LINDY Oh yeh?
JOSIE When Jason and me picked you up at Newport
   Pagnell, I said what's a girl like you doing on the
   road. He's given lifts to all sorts. That's what he
   said. Only I'm different.

> LINDY *looks at the blouse.*

LINDY What's that?
JOSIE Don't you listen? It's my blouse. Jason said some
   kids only do it for the kicks. I couldn't do that. Well
   I mean, I know I didn't get off at London . . . but . . .
   well Jason and me clicked right off. When we get
   back to London though . . . I'll find a place and then
   maybe he'll come and see me on his trips. I could
   settle down with someone like Jason.

LINDY Maybe you should listen to that girl. She's been on the road for years.

JOSIE How do you know?

LINDY I know.

> LINDY *tidies herself up a bit. She's ready to go.*

LINDY How old are you, Josie?

JOSIE Eighteen.

LINDY No you're not. How old d'you think I am?

JOSIE I dunno. Twenty. Twenty one?

LINDY I'll be fifteen next Sunday.

JOSIE Thirteen then. I'm thirteen. So what?

LINDY Do you want some stuff?

JOSIE Eh . . . OK. Try anything once.

LINDY Well, not this time. You have to work for it. I just used the last. You don't get free offers in this game.

JOSIE Oh I know.

> LINDY *picks up her bag.*

LINDY I'll just see if Jason's ready, shall I?

JOSIE Right. Tell him I'll be right there.

LINDY Take your time.

> LINDY *leaves.* JOSIE *puts her shoes on. Then she gets her blouse and puts that on. She rummages in her bag and finds some postcards. Maybe she'll send a few. She searches for her biro. She sits and thinks. But there's no one to send a postcard to. She*

throws them into the bin. She looks in the mirror, stands tall and smiles at herself. Then she goes out. JOSIE *comes storming in again and flings her bag at the wall. She sits down and howls.*

JOSIE The sods. The mean sods.

A CLEANER *with a mop, cloth and bucket comes in.* JOSIE *ignores her. The* CLEANER *goes into the lavatory used by* LINDY. *She comes out with a twisted syringe.*

CLEANER Good thing I wear rubber gloves. Is this yours?
JOSIE What? No.
CLEANER Flaming kids.

She goes back into the lavatory. JOSIE *gets up and looks in the mirror. She wipes away her tears. After a moment she looks for her lipstick. She puts some on and presses her lips together. Then she scrawls 'Up Yours' on the mirror. She leaves. The* CLEANER *comes out of the lavatory and cleans the mirror as if she's done it all before.*

SLAVE!
MYLES ECKERSLEY

Characters

JONAS THE JUMPER	
QUAKER OATS	a Quaker farmer
LORD HENRY SOMERSETT	Aristocrat
SIR FREDERICK FERNLEY, K.C.	Barrister
LADY ADDELINE SOMERSETT	Henry's wife
SIR GRANVILLE SHARP, K.C.	Barrister
JONES	Granville Sharp's assistant
EDWARD SOMERSETT	Negro slave boy
COURTENAY CLARK	Clerk of the Court
LORD MANSFIELD	Judge
THUGS, JURYMEN, GAOLERS	
SLAVES, PRISONERS	
ATTENDANTS TO LADY SOMERSETT	

The action takes place in England in 1771 in His Majesty's Quarter Sessions, The Courthouse, prison and so forth.

The Georgian era was a vigorous time when very few people had any formal education. Disease, neglect, cruelty and ignorance abounded, as well as a great capacity to live life to the full. Contrasted with the more natural, coarse side of humanity, there was the world of the Gentlemen and the Ladies, where wealth, position, style and manners were everything.

Behind all this was the growing wealth of Britain and her colonies: the Industrial Revolution was just beginning. It was a time of social upheaval with thousands being without any homes or means of livelihood.

And it was the time of the Slave Trade. Britain did very well out of the Slave Trade, which had been going on for over a hundred years. The ports of Bristol and Liverpool grew rich on this trade.

Slave ships were of about 230 tons, and could carry 500 slaves, squashed in side by side.

The slave captains would pick up the slaves from traders on the Gold Coast, in Africa, and sail across the Atlantic to America. The slaves were sold in America, and cotton, tobacco and sugar brought back to England. It was a good trade, and those involved were reluctant to have anything change it.

In the play there are three main groups:
    The Pro-slavery group
    The Anti-slavery group
    and the Law

The first group, the *Pros*, represent the majority with Lord Somersett at its head. His assistant Jonas represents the henchmen who carry out his orders and keep the peace, by the whip and the lash.

The second group, the *Antis*, are in a minority. The Anti-Slavery Society was formed in England to try and stop slavery. Wilberforce was one of its most effective members. The slave trade was made illegal in 1803 and slavery abolished in the British Empire in 1833. It took considerably longer, and a war, to stop slavery in America.

Oats represents the Quakers who did a lot in America to help the slaves by letting them escape into Canada.

The third group is the Law. The Law was sacrosanct to the Georgians, because there was so much unrest. There was hunger and poverty as land was being 'enclosed' for better farming leaving many ordinary people without their livelihood. People left the land in search of work in factories, but still there was great hunger and poverty. 'To be hung for a sheep as for a lamb' became a true statement. Offences such as stealing were punished by hanging, or transportation. The prison hulks in the Thames and Portsmouth harbour were full to bursting with so-called felons, whose main crime was to be destitute, and desperate. The set should be as simple as possible, but can be elaborated if means are available. A good chair for the Judge, chairs for the *Antis* on the right, benches for the *Pros* on the left, and a box for the prisoner. Various tables and chairs for the *Law*.

> JONAS THE JUMPER *enters with a gang of thugs, carrying whips.*

JONAS Right then – none of you move – keep still!
  Know this! We are the jumpers, we make you jump!
  Don't move – or we will make you jump so high you will freeze!
  You'll be seeing us,
  Again, and again, and again!

> *They go out with a flourish and a whiplash or*
> *two.* OATS *appears. Looks about fearfully. He*
> *is not one of nature's athletes, thin and a bit*
> *uncoordinated, falling over things easily. His*
> *appearance belies his character, a man who*
> *supports the underdog. He is a Quaker and*
> *wears a black hat.*

OATS [*Frightened*] Have they gone? He frightens me,
he does, that Jonas. Acts the big oaf! My name is
Oats, Ezekiel Oats. I have a little farm in America,
and I have my family home here, in England, which I
am visiting. It is 1771, and King George the Third is
on the throne. Let's begin with My Lord Somersett.

> LORD SOMERSETT *enters with a great flourish*
> *and strides across the stage. He wears a very*
> *large hat with a large ostrich feather in it.*

Fat, fiendish and fierce! Notice the size of his hat. He
owns much land and money. Also, he owns people,
slaves, from Africa.

SOMERSETT Oats, what are you doin' here?

OATS [*Bowing*] Just going, my Lord. [*To audience*]
His Lordship has estates, one here in England, and a
huge one in Virginia. That's in America, one of our
Colonies.

SOMERSETT Oats! When are you goin' orf?

OATS [*To audience*] Notice that his Lordship has
trouble in pronouncin' – I mean, pronouncing – his
INGS. He says, floggin', hangin' and whoopin' corff.

SOMERSETT Orff! Oats, go!

OATS Yes, my Lord. The story so far. His Lordship and his wife have come to England, for a holiday. They live mostly in Virginia. When they come to England they bring with them their servants and their slaves. A black negro slave, a page-boy, called Edward, has run away. Run off, just like that. Of course he was very soon recaptured; you can't hide with that kind of a face for long. He is now in Newgate gaol awaiting his trial; they just might hang him!

SOMERSETT Oats! Out! [OATS *goes out quickly*]

> SIR FREDERICK FERNLEY *enters, a barrister with a wig and gown, a mean-looking man with short sight and specs.*

You are late Fernley!

> FERNLEY *peers closely at papers.*

FERNLEY Yes, yes, sorry, my Lord, delayed – at court. This boy. [*He peers again*] Ah, Edward Somersett. I have to tell you that he is in Newgate Prison.

SOMERSETT [*Impatient*] Yes, you idiot! I put him there – and I paid my fees for him.

FERNLEY I see, I see. Well, I have bad news for you; none other than Sir Granville Barker Sharp is undertaking his defence.

SOMERSETT [*Mouth falls open*] What? What? Him! I don't believe it! How does a slave boy get the best lawyer in the country?

FERNLEY [*Coughs*] The second best lawyer in the country, my Lord. It seems that [*He peers at paper close to his eyes*] the Anti-Slavery Society has put up the money.

SOMERSETT What! Those wets are ruining the country!

FERNLEY Yes, they are ruining the country.

SOMERSETT Fernley, I want the boy convicted. I want the boy condemned to be flogged, branded on his black hide, and sold to a devil of an owner. He doesn't know when he is well orf! Have him convicted, Fernley!

FERNLEY My Lord, I will do my best.

SOMERSETT [*Eagerly*] Any chance of gettin' the brat hung?

FERNLEY Judge Mansfield likes hanging. He topped fifty last year.

SOMERSETT Nothin' like a good hangin'; the crowd love it, and they will love this one, a black boy.

FERNLEY But . . . [*He sounds doubtful about hanging*]

SOMERSETT No 'Buts', Fernley, for me no buts!

LADY SOMERSETT *enters, a handsome woman, in a large flowered hat. Her retinue of maids and black pages present a colourful picture.*

LADY SOMERSETT No buts! You could do with a good butt, Bungey; I even know a good old nanny goat to give you one!

SOMERSETT Are you offerin', my dear? [*The retinue laugh*]

LADY SOMERSETT No, but try Sir Frederick, I am told he butts with the best of the nanny goats!

SOMERSETT Quite so! My dear, have you heard? Those Anti-Slavery wets have put up the money for that runaway boy, Edward. What about that, eh?

LADY SOMERSETT I know, I put up the money myself.

SOMERSETT [*Mouth falls open*] What! You stupid woman! That was my money! You have no right!

LADY SOMERSETT No, it was my money I used. I have my own money, Bungey, don't forget that!

SOMERSETT You cannot do this, my dear! You will ruin us, all of us! Think what you are doing. [*In hushed voice*] We have to hang on to our slaves at all costs! Why did you do it?

LADY SOMERSETT I have had a think. I brought that boy up; it was largely my fault that he ran away.

SOMERSETT What!

LADY SOMERSETT He was far too intelligent to go on as he was.

SOMERSETT O yes you spoilt him. I know that; you always do spoil your brats, and that includes my sons as well! You won't get away with this! Tell her, Fernley.

FERNLEY [*Meanly*] Well, my Lady. There is very little chance of the boy getting off. He has been charged with many charges, some of which are capital offences. I mention just one, for which he can be hung. [*He peers closely at paper*] The Waltham Black Act, section 9. 'Appearing with a sooty face on the Highway.'

LADY SOMERSETT What? But the boy is naturally sooty.

FERNLEY I cannot help that, the Law is the Law, and a sooty face is an offence. The Law has to be upheld in this time of thieves, robbers, muggers, rapists and agents of anarchy. We must defend ourselves against those who want to destroy our way of life.

SIR GRANVILLE SHARP *enters, a fine-looking person, he too wears a wig and gown. He is followed by his Welsh assistant,* JONES AP JONES.

LADY SOMERSETT Sir Granville Sharp, how nice to see
you.

SIR GRANVILLE [*Bows deeply*] Your Ladyship. [*He
kisses her hand*]

SOMERSETT Sir Granville Barker Sharp! [*He bites out
each word*] How dare you demean us all by
defending that black brat! You, Sir, are a traitor!
Come, Fernley, before I do something violent!

> SOMERSETT *exits followed by a fussy* FERNLEY.

SIR GRANVILLE O dear, it appears that your husband is
upset. Now, to the slave boy. I cannot give you much
hope that he will get off. There is too much at stake
here.

LADY SOMERSETT But you will try, Granville, won't
you? I have such great faith in you. [*She turns to the
retinue*] Haven't we?

ALL Yes!

LADY SOMERSETT Get Edward off and you will be well
rewarded, Sir Granville.

> As SIR GRANVILLE *bows she goes out with her
retinue.*

SIR GRANVILLE Well, what do you think of her, eh?
Jones ap Jones —

JONES A fine a piece of porcelain as I have seen for
many a day. A case worth winning, Sir Granville.

SIR GRANVILLE For the reward you mean? [*He
ponders*] You are a wicked fellow, Jones, if I think
what you are thinking.

JONES From that cup you drink a lovely cup of cocoa,
Sir.

SIR GRANVILLE Quite so.

> *They go out.* JONAS *enters with the thug*
> *pushing the manacled page-boy* EDWARD. *He*
> *wears a frilly shirt, velvet breeches.*

JONAS Now boy, your trial is coming up. [*To thugs*]
The shirt! [*They hold up a filthy dirty shirt*] His
Lordship requires that you wear this uniform today,
since you spurn the other one!

> *The thugs take off the frilly shirt and put on*
> *the filthy one. They pull off the velvet*
> *breeches.*

That's better, more like a monkey, eh? Now, His
Lordship don't want you displaying your gifts of
speech, what I gather you have been training in. I
think your monkey brain has picked up the readin'
and the writin'! Forget that! We don't want no talk
in court, get it! You say 'Haaaa' for 'Yes', and
'Moooo' for 'No' – see. Now, you say, 'Yes'.

EDWARD Yes, Sir.

THUG 'Haaaaaa.'

EDWARD Oh, I see – 'Haaaaaaa' Sir.

JONAS No 'Sir'! Now, say 'No'!

EDWARD Moooooo.

THUGS [*Echo*] Moooooo. [*They fling him to the*
ground]

JONAS That's enough boys, very good, monkey – and
you remember, eh, monkey! Don't go away, we shall
be back.

THUGS Again, and again, and again! Monkey!

> EDWARD *slumps down and sobs.* THE CLERK OF
> THE COURT *enters.* FERNLEY, SIR GRANVILLE, *and*
> ATTENDANTS *enter.* SOMERSETT *enters and sits*
> *to the left side.* LADY SOMERSETT *and* RETINUE
> *enter, and sit to the right.* JONAS AND THE
> THUGS *take* EDWARD *to the prisoner's box.*
> *They and other supporters join* SIR SHARP. LORD
> MANSFIELD *enters and goes to his central chair.*

CLERK All rise! [*They stand*]
Here ye, here ye! His Majesty King George the
Third, His Quarter Sessions, in the years 1771. Case
number 5. Edward Somersett, negro slave; you are
charged under Sections 9, 10 and 69 of the Law and
Order Act (1765) and Sections 3, 8 and 89 of the
Law and Order Act (1768). How do you plead?
[*They all sit*]

SIR GRANVILLE My Lord, may I submit a point of Law?

MANSFIELD [*Surprised*] Is it pertinent, and brief? I do
like brevity.

SIR GRANVILLE Quite so, my Lord, most commendable.

MANSFIELD Your submission?

SIR GRANVILLE Is simple. I submit to you that there is
no case to be submitted.

FERNLEY [*Leaps up*] My Lord, this is preposterous!

MANSFIELD Yes, it may well be so, but let us hear what
is to be said.

SIR GRANVILLE Simply, that there is no Law which
permits slavery in this country. That means that this
boy was perfectly entitled to come and go as he
pleased.

SOMERSETT [*Leaps up*] Poppycock!

JONAS AND CROWD Rubbish!

CLERK Silence! Silence!

MANSFIELD I shall send interruptors to prison if there is
  any more noise. Sit down, my Lord. [*They all sit*] Sir
  Frederick, please help me submit your reasons for
  bringing this case.

FERNLEY My Lord. [*He presents paper*] Virginia, in
  America, is one of His Majesty's Colonies. The Law,
  in Virginia, permits slavery. Parliament, in
  Whitehall, permits the Colonial Office to administer
  Virginia for us. Parliament sanctions their Laws. We
  are duty bound to uphold their Laws, because their
  Laws are Parliament's Laws. The Colony of
  Virginia, through its Governor General and its
  councils, sees that the Law is kept. We are duty
  bound to uphold their Laws; we made them.

MANSFIELD [*Peeved*] I like not being told to be duty
  bound to do anything, in my Court. I am the Law
  here, Sir Frederick.

LADY SOMERSETT AND RETINUE Hurrah!

JONAS AND THUGS Rubbish!

CLERK Silence!

MANSFIELD In view of this disturbance, I feel it is time
  for a recess. I shall consider this matter, and we shall
  reconvene in due course. [*He gets up*]

CLERK All rise! [*They all get up. His Lordship leaves*]

> *The crowd goes out leaving only* JONAS, *the*
> THUGS, EDWARD *and* SIR GRANVILLE.

SIR GRANVILLE I wish to speak to the boy alone.

JONAS [*Self-importantly*] You should have an
  authorisation from the Clerk, Sir.

SIR GRANVILLE I have. [*He offers* JONAS *a bag of coins*]

JONAS Thank you sir. We have business – in the
  Tavern, Sir.

> *They all go out leaving* EDWARD *and* SIR
> GRANVILLE.

SIR GRANVILLE I think we have won round one. I want
you to tell me more than you already have. Am I a
bit frightening for you?

EDWARD O no, Sir. I am used to people like you, Sir. In
my Lady's house we meet all kinds of grand people. I
have even met the King, as a page-boy, of course.

SIR GRANVILLE Lady Somersett has given me a very
good report of you. Tell me about her.

EDWARD She is a kind lady; she has taught me many
things.

SIR GRANVILLE Yes?

EDWARD Like writing, reading, spelling, drawing. I
was taught along with her sons and daughters. There
were tutors and governesses.

SIR GRANVILLE I see. Don't you think it was wrong of
you to run away, after all she had done for you.

EDWARD No, sir.

SIR GRANVILLE You could be considered an ungrateful
boy, couldn't you?

EDWARD No.

SIR GRANVILLE No? Why did you run away?

EDWARD She understands. I didn't run from her, I ran
away from being a slave. That's what I ran from!

SIR GRANVILLE I see. You came from Africa. You were
shipped on the *Orion*, a slaver of 240 tons, carrying
550 slaves and 40 crew. Do you remember that
voyage?

EDWARD Only a little, sir.

SIR GRANVILLE Describe your memories.

EDWARD There was a place for us children, a kind of
cage, in the middle of the ship. We were chained

together, so close, we could not move. I remember that the boy next to me died one night. There was more room to move as more and more died.

SIR GRANVILLE So, if I mention to the Court that of the 500 slaves loaded, only 200 survived, you could say that?

EDWARD No, I don't know how many died.

> A GROUP OF SLAVES *enters and lies down close together, chains clanking.*

We weren't even given buckets. The smell was terrible. The bread was full of maggots. [THE THUGS *bring bread*] And sometimes we went up on deck [*They mime walking*] and they would throw water at us [*They mime buckets of water being thrown*] to clean us. [*They are swabbed with mops*] It was then that they could remove the dead bodies [*They mime picking up bodies*] and fling them into the sea. Then, when we got across the sea, we were put in a ring to be sold.

> THE SLAVES *go into a ring;* THE THUGS *push them about.* LORD SOMERSETT *enters with* JONAS. *They look into the mouths of the children and feel them as if they were cattle.* JONAS *places a chair in the ring and* EDWARD *is put on the chair. An auctioneer stands to one side.*

AUCTIONEER Now Gentlemen, let's us get to Lot number 1. An African slave boy, aged, about 4 years. Good limbs, sound mover, no disease and from a well-recommended area.

> A THUG *makes* EDWARD *run up and down, and jump several times.* LORD SOMERSETT *inspects his eyes, ears, limbs and feet.*

A sound boy, there, my Lord. Now what do I hear, three guineas? Three guineas, three guineas, do I hear three guineas? [*Bidder bids*] Thank you! At three and a half, do I hear three and a half? [*Bid*] Thank you, four guineas, four guineas, four and a half, at four and a half, four and a half, four and a half, five, five, five. [*A bid*] Thank you, this boy is very sound, as you can see – five and a half? Five and a half. [*There is no bid*] I shall have to let it go at Five. At five, five. [*Bang*] Somersett.

> OATS *enters.*

OATS And Edward went to Lord Somersett's Estate, where cotton was grown. He was taken into domestic service and became a Silver Rubber. This meant he helped the Silver Butler to polish the silver. That was alright until the Silver Butler was promoted. The new Silver Butler did not like Edward, and one day complained about Edward to the Head Butler, who took the complaint to his Lordship. It was said Edward did not clean the silver properly.

> JONAS *enters with* THE THUGS, *carrying whips.*

These men are the Jumpers, professional punishers. The Plantation owners hire them, when they need them, to flog their slaves who have been reported for misbehaviour. His Lordship gives them a list of names, and the number of lashes to be administered.

[JONAS *holds up the list.*]

JONAS Edward Somersett, laziness, 50 lashes.

OATS [*Protesting to* JONAS] But the boy is only twelve, you will kill him!

JONAS Look mate, we don't kill no one, we know our job; anyway, they don't feel it like we do, they are just animals. Leave it to us; we know what we are doing, we are experts, we are.

[JONAS *goes out with* THE THUGS *and* EDWARD.]

OATS They take their customers into the fields behind the sheds, where their screams cannot be heard by sensitive ears. You will hear nothing, feel nothing. They say a flogging is over soon enough. Such is our madness!

[LADY SOMERSETT *enters looking very concerned, with a maid.*]

LADY SOMERSETT Have the Jumpers been?

OATS Yes, my Lady.

LADY SOMERSETT And did they flog Edward, the Silver Rubber?

OATS Yes.

LADY SOMERSETT O my God! The savages! I must see my husband about this, at once. I will never allow it again! Ever!

[*She goes out.*]

OATS And the boy was taken into the care of her Ladyship.

MAID He was dressed up in fine breeches and a green jacket, [EDWARD *enters in velvet breeches and a frilly shirt. The maid helps him on with his jacket*] and black buckle shoes! [*The shoes go on*] What a fine sight he was!

OATS And as time went by, his education made him something special. He had a fine intelligence . . .

MAID and a fine physique; he was something of a favourite with Lady Somersett, and with us.

OATS Even Lord Somersett showed some interest in him, a fact that was hard for Edward to bear, but he tried.

> OATS *and* THE MAID *go out as* LADY SOMERSETT *enters, holding a paper.*

LADY SOMERSETT Edward, did you do this?

EDWARD Yes, my Lady.

LADY SOMERSETT It's very well copied, in such excellent writing. You have been reading Shakespeare. He is a good writer to copy. You don't have to do all this dedication to me.

EDWARD I wanted to.

LADY SOMERSETT Edward, you are fifteen years old now, and growing up. You must remember, you are still a slave.

EDWARD How can I forget? I do sometimes, but then, someone always reminds me, someone with a white face.

LADY SOMERSETT My sons are not pleased with you; they think you are getting too . . .

EDWARD big for my black boots, they told me.

LADY SOMERSETT Be careful with them, Edward.

EDWARD But I am. I always try to give way to them.
But they can't beat me at running and jumping –
only if I let them, which I do sometimes.

LADY SOMERSETT You are learning diplomacy,
Edward, good. All the same, I think it better now, if
you did not have too much to do with them. They
are going to school, and are changing.

EDWARD I noticed.

LADY SOMERSETT Edward, it is your birthday, what
present would you like?

EDWARD You will laugh if I tell you.

LADY SOMERSETT No.

EDWARD I want to stand alone, in an English field and
see the dawn come. I want the sun to cover me, and I
shall be free. And, nobody shall say, 'Slave, come
here'.

LADY SOMERSETT [*Alarmed*] No, Edward. Oh dear,
what have I done? You cannot stand anywhere,
alone, it's impossible.

EDWARD But you could let me.

LADY SOMERSETT No, I could not. The whole system
forbids it. Everyone, black or white, would be down
on me like so many hungry hawks. To break the
code is wrong.

EDWARD Then why did you have me educated? Why?
[*He is almost in tears*] Why can't I just go in to that
field? It's not much to ask.

LADY SOMERSETT Edward, take a grip on yourself.
Don't give way. You must wait; we shall free you
one day, you see!

EDWARD One day? Which day? My funeral day?

LADY SOMERSETT Now Edward, it is time you went
about your business. You must forget this idea,
promise? [*She hands him the sonnet*] You keep this.

EDWARD I don't want it! [*He tears it up.*]

LADY SOMERSETT Edward! That was a bad thing to do! You have so much to learn, please learn, for my sake. [*She kisses him gently on the cheek.* LADY SOMERSETT *goes out as* EDWARD *bows.*]

> EDWARD *stands as if trying to make up his mind. Then, he goes out running.*
>
> OATS *enters and trips up.*

OATS Oh bother – Edward went missing at 4 o'clock in the afternoon, and was not seen until the following day.

> *The light dims as* EDWARD *enters. He stands centre stage, as the light simulates dawn. He holds up his arms; he greets the sun, alone and free.*
>
> THE THUGS *enters, chase him and he is bundled off.*
>
> THE CLERK OF THE COURT *enters, followed by* FERNLEY, SHARP *and* ATTENDANTS. LADY SOMERSETT *enters with retinue and crowd.* JONAS *puts* EDWARD *into the box.*

THUGS Hang the boy!

CROWD Blackie!

RETINUE Let him go free! Free him! Free him!

CLERK Silence! [LORD MANSFIELD *enters; he is a bit unsteady. He has had a heavy night of port wine and carousal*] All rise! [*They rise*]

> *He sits down as he fumbles with the papers.*

MANSFIELD Mister Clerk, it is the Slave boy case, isn't it? [THE CLERK *nods*] Yes, it's the sentence, isn't it?

CLERK [*Hisses*] No Lord, the OPINION, the ruling!

MANSFIELD Yes, yes. I see. [*He looks for more papers*] Quite a bad night I had. [*He reads a bit*] Yes – I have given some time to considering this case. I have weighed up the arguments for the prosecution and the defence. It is now my duty to pass sentence. [*He puts on the black hat.* THE CLERK *leaps up and puts a paper in front of him.*]

CLERK No, my Lord. *Not* the black hat, just the OPINION.

> THE JUDGE *removes black hat and takes up the paper.*

MANSFIELD Right.

SOMERSETT [*Leaping up*] Hang the boy!

JONAS AND CROWD Hang him! Hang him! Hang him!

CLERK Silence!

MANSFIELD If there is not quiet in this court I shall hang you, my Lord. This outburst is most unseemly [*He rubs his head*] and uncomfortable.

> *He takes up paper.*

We do sanction slavery in our Colonies. Nevertheless, I have taken advice from every quarter, and there is no sanction whatever of any

Law which permits Slavery in this country of Great Britain and Ireland. Therefore it is my opinion that there is no case here, I have therefore decided to DISMISS THE CASE. I so rule!

> *He stands uncertainly and hobbles out.*
>
> *There's stunned silence. Suddenly pandemonium breaks out.*

LADY SOMERSETT AND RETINUE Three cheers for his Lordship, hoorah, hoorah, hoorah!

JONAS AND THUGS Rubbish! [*They start to overturn the benches; there is chaos*]

> FERNLEY *and* THE CLERK *are engulfed in protesters including* LORD SOMERSETT.
>
> OATS *goes to* EDWARD *and his supporters lift him up, in triumph.*
>
> THE THUGS *don't like this; they attack.*
>
> SIR GRANVILLE *fires a pistol shot into the air.*

SIR GRANVILLE Ladies and gentlemen, let us be calm. [*He holds in his hand many gold coins*] Let us not brawl! Here! [*He throws coins*] Let us celebrate! Or drown your sorrows in Gin! It is cheap! Good health to you all!

> *There is general cheering as they gather up the coins and rush off to drink.*
>
> *A conveyance enters to take* LADY SOMERSETT *off with* SIR GRANVILLE. LORD SOMERSETT *stumps off.*

JONES And if you are wondering where they are off to, so am I! We get our just rewards! [*He goes out with the maid.* EDWARD *is left standing alone with* OATS.]

EDWARD Now what, I am free, I am free, I am free.

OATS Look happier, Edward; it could have been so much worse for you.

EDWARD What now?

OATS I know of a family who are looking for a Silver Butler. Would you like that? They are a good Quaker family; they will be good to you. You do know about silver, don't you?

EDWARD Yes Sir.

OATS Nay, don't 'Sir' me, Edward. I am your friend.

EDWARD But still a slave, really.

OATS You will take this job?

EDWARD Yes, and thank you, my friend. [*He hugs him*] I am not a slave any more, am I?

OATS You cannot go back to Virginia; they will crucify you if you do.

EDWARD Why can't I go back with Lady Somersett?

OATS It is impossible; you must understand that.

EDWARD I can now stand in a field, alone, and free.

OATS Don't be unhappy, Edward, make the best of it.

EDWARD I will – I will –
I might go back to Africa –
[*He shakes his head*]
But I never will.

A MESSAGE FROM THE OTHER SIDE
JOYCE HOLLIDAY

Characters

MUM	aged early forties, fussy, active, a worrier
SARAH	aged 14/15, fussy, active, a worrier
JOANNE	aged 14/15, a natural leader
MICHAEL	around 10, an opportunist
JULIE	aged 14/15, attractive, excitable, a bit silly, bossy
DAWN	aged 14/15, slow, passive, with under-currents
GAS	aged 16/17, out of his depth
MRS PROCTOR	aged 60s, a nosy-parker

Some people believe very strongly in a spirit world where the dead are waiting with messages for us if we will only listen, and others think that's nonsense. But whether you start off trying to contact 'the other side' as a serious experiment or just as a bit of fun, it can easily become quite frightening. Who knows what evil spirits are lurking out there and what they may do to you? You don't have to go to Dracula's castle or sleep in a graveyard to scare yourself silly.

> *A living-room with table and chairs.*
> *Late Autumn, evening.*
> JOANNE *is sitting, reading a book.* SARAH *comes on from one direction, carrying a coat.*
> MICHAEL *trails behind her.* MUM *comes on from the other direction with food.*

SARAH Here's your coat, mum.

MUM Thanks. Oh dear, I am going to be late. Here are some crisps for you and some chocolate biscuits. Now, where did I put my shoes?

> MUM *goes off again.* SARAH *puts the coat over a chair and goes to whisper to* JOANNE. MICHAEL *tries to listen.*

SARAH She's nearly half an hour late already.

JOANNE What time are they coming?

SARAH Any minute. I said eight o'clock.

JOANNE It's nearly eight o'clock now.

SARAH I know it is. That's what I just said.

JOANNE Don't get ratty with me.

SARAH She said she was going out at half past seven. I thought eight o'clock'd be safe.

MICHAEL Who's coming at eight o'clock?

SARAH Nobody.

MICHAEL You said . . .

SARAH Don't you dare breathe a word. I'll murder you if you do.

> MUM *comes back in with her shoes on.*

MUM Where did you put my coat?

> SARAH *points to the chair.* MUM *puts her coat on.*

MUM Now, are you going to be alright?

SARAH Yes, mum.

MUM And you've got the telephone number in case there's an emergency?

SARAH Yes, mum.

MUM And you will go to Mrs Proctor's to use her telephone if anything goes wrong?

SARAH She's such a nosy-parker.

MUM Well, I don't want you going right down the street on your own in the dark. And that one on the corner's bound to be out of order. Do be sensible.

SARAH Yes, mum.

MUM And, Michael, you be a good boy, won't you, and go to bed when it's your bedtime? No arguing.

MICHAEL Mum, who's coming?

> SARAH *kicks him.*

MUM Nobody's coming, love, except Joanne. She's staying the night with Sarah while I go out. You know that. Now, I'd better be off. Oh, my handbag! Where did I put my handbag?

> MUM *goes off again.*

SARAH They'll be here.

JOANNE [*Putting down her book and jumping up*] I'll go and stop them.

SARAH Oh, yes. If you can. Oh, please.

> JOANNE *off in one direction.* MUM *back on from the other.*

MUM I put it on the bed. [*Looking in bag*] Now, have I got everything? Where's Joanne gone?

SARAH Joanne? Oh, she just . . .

MICHAEL She's gone out to . . .

> SARAH *manages to shut him up.*

MUM [*Abstractedly, still searching in her bag*] Gone out?

SARAH She's gone to the shop. To buy some coke.

MUM I already got you a bottle – in the pantry. I don't like her going out like that.

SARAH She'll be all right.

MUM Now, I expect you'll be fast asleep when I come back, so, goodnight, love. [*Kisses her*] And night, night, Michael. Be a good little boy. [*Kisses him*] Right, I'm off.

> *She starts to go, then pauses in the doorway.*

MUM You're sure you'll be alright?

SARAH Mum, just go.

> MUM *shrugs and goes.* SARAH *breathes a huge sigh of relief.*

MICHAEL You told fibs.

SARAH Not really.

MICHAEL Yes, you did.

SARAH Don't you dare say anything.

MICHAEL I want some crisps.

SARAH You don't deserve anything, you little . . .

MICHAEL I shall tell mum.

SARAH What will you tell her?

MICHAEL Who is it who's coming?

SARAH Nobody. And it's your bedtime.

MICHAEL No, it isn't. I'm not going to bed yet. It's not
time. I'm going to stay up late and have some crisps.

SARAH You can have a whole packet to yourself, if you
go to bed now.

MICHAEL Two packets.

SARAH [*Grudgingly*] Alright, two packets. But you've
got to go now.

MICHAEL And the chocolate biscuits.

SARAH Oh, take them! But go to bed now.

> MICHAEL, *clutching his loot, goes towards the
> door.*

MICHAEL I'm not going to sleep yet.

SARAH You can read in bed for half an hour.

MICHAEL An hour.

SARAH Alright, an hour! But go to bed now!

> *She pushes him out and follows him to check
> that he's gone.* JOANNE *enters.*

JOANNE Sarah, we're here! Sarah? Sarah!

> DAWN *and* JULIE *enter, giggling.*

JULIE She made us get down behind a wall.

> SARAH *returns.*

SARAH Not so loud. I don't want Michael to hear you.
JULIE Who's Michael?
SARAH He's my little brother. He'd tell my mum.
DAWN Your mum must be ever so fierce.
SARAH No. She's not. She's nice.
JULIE Well, why did we have to hide behind the wall then? I got my shoes all muddy.
DAWN I lost my ear-ring.
SARAH It's just that I didn't tell her. She doesn't go out a lot.
JULIE [*Speaking to someone off*] Come on. It's all right.
JOANNE [*To Sarah*] She's gone and brought Gas with her.
SARAH Oh, no. What's she brought him for?

> GAS *stands awkwardly in the doorway,*
> *carrying some cans.*

JULIE It *is* all right if Gas comes, isn't it? We've brought some cider and stuff.
SARAH I suppose so.
JULIE I said it'd be all right, didn't I? Come in properly.
GAS Do we have to?
JULIE Yes. This is going to be exciting. We're going to put all the lights out and sit in the dark and . . .

DAWN Do we have to sit in the dark?

JULIE Of course we do. You can't do it properly unless it's dark.

DAWN I don't like the dark.

JULIE That's the exciting part.

SARAH We're going to have a candle. I'll fetch it now.

> SARAH *off*.

JOANNE Right. Pull this table out so we can sit round it.

JULIE Come on, Gas. Move the table.

GAS Oh, no . . .

JULIE Where shall we put it?

JOANNE Put it here. No, not here. Here!

GAS [*Moaning*] Oh . . .

JOANNE Put the chairs round.

> *They do as they are told.* JOANNE *sits down.*

JOANNE I'll write out the letters of the alphabet.

> SARAH *returns.*

SARAH Here's the candle.

JOANNE Put it in the middle of the table. And we shall need a glass.

SARAH A glass. Right. I'll go and get a glass.

> SARAH *goes off again.*

DAWN It's alright. We can drink out of the cans.

JOANNE It's to put our hands on.

DAWN Is that how it works?

JULIE We all put our hands on the glass and it moves. It's really spooky.

DAWN I don't think I should have come.

JULIE Oh, don't be so dreary, Dawn.

SARAH *returns*.

SARAH One glass.

JOANNE Put it in the middle of the table. And we shall need some scissors.

SARAH Scissors. Right. I'll go and get some scissors.

SARAH *goes off again*.

JOANNE And we shall need another chair for Gas.

GAS No, I don't want . . .

JOANNE I saw a stool in the kitchen.

JULIE Gas, go and get the stool.

GAS Can't we go?

JULIE No. I want to stay here. I've always wanted to do this. So, shut up and fetch the stool.

SARAH *returns*.

SARAH Here's the scissors.

JULIE Give them here. I'll cut the letters out. Give me a page, Joanne.

JOANNE Can Gas have the stool from the kitchen? It's through there.

> GAS *goes reluctantly.* JOANNE *still writing.* JULIE *cutting.*

SARAH I wonder if it'll work.

JULIE What are we going to ask it?

JOANNE Whatever we want. There must be something you'd like to know.

DAWN I'd like to know where my ear-ring is.

JOANNE You can't ask things like that, Dawn. They've got to be important things.

DAWN My ear-ring is important to me.

JULIE Here, Dawn, put them out. Put them in a circle.

> DAWN *fiddles with the letters.*

SARAH Shall I light the candle yet?

JOANNE Not till we're ready.

JULIE We need a 'yes' and a 'no' as well.

JOANNE [*Writing*] Yes. No. Where do you put those?

JULIE Oh, Dawn, you're supposed to put them in alphabetical order. You are useless.

SARAH I'll do them.

> GAS *returns with the stool.*

GAS Where shall I put it?

JULIE Over here. Put it over here, next to me.

> GAS *does as he is told.*

JOANNE Are we all ready now?

SARAH Nearly.

GAS D'you want a can?

JULIE Not yet. We're too busy. We're just going to start.

GAS Well, I do.

[GAS *opens a can.*]

JULIE You sprayed it all over me!

GAS Sorry.

SARAH There, that'll do.

JOANNE Right. Light the candle then. I'll put the light out.

JULIE Have you got a match, Gas? Ooh, isn't this exciting!

GAS Here. Anybody want a fag?

[GAS *passes his matches to* JULIE *who lights the candle.*]

JULIE No. Not now.

GAS Well, I do.

SARAH My mum won't have smoking in the house.

DAWN Your mum's not here.

SARAH She'll smell it when she comes back. She can always smell it.

JULIE You can manage without a fag for ten minutes, Gas.

GAS Oh . . .

[GAS *puts his fags away and guzzles his beer.*]

SARAH That's got a funny smell for cider.

GAS That's 'cos it's beer.

SARAH I don't think my Mum . . .

JOANNE Are we all ready? Lights out!

DAWN I'm frightened.

JULIE Shut up, Dawn.

DAWN What if it gets us?

JOANNE What if what gets us?

DAWN Whatever it is.

JULIE Don't be stupid, Dawn.

JOANNE Now. All put your hands on the glass.

SARAH The candle's in the way. We can't move the glass round the candle.

JOANNE Put the candle over there then.

DAWN I'm frightened of the dark.

JOANNE Put the candle next to Dawn then.

> *They move the candle.*

JOANNE Right. All put your hands on the glass.

JULIE Come on, Gas. You as well.

GAS Do I have to?

JULIE Course you do. Doesn't he?

SARAH I suppose so.

> GAS *reluctantly joins in.*

JULIE What shall we ask it?

SARAH We've all got to be quiet first and concentrate.

> *They concentrate.* DAWN *whimpers slightly,*
> JULIE *gives a very little giggle,* GAS *a very small*
> *snort of disapproval.*

SARAH Quiet!

JOANNE [*Slowly and dramatically*] Is there anybody there?

SARAH It moved!

JULIE It's moved to 'yes'!

DAWN Who is it?

JOANNE Who are you? What is your name?

SARAH M

JULIE It's spelling it out!

SARAH A

DAWN I'm frightened!

SARAH R

JOANNE And Y . . . Mary! It's called Mary!

SARAH L . . . I

JOANNE N . . . Lin . . . Do you think it's Linton like Wuthering Heights?

SARAH M . . . Shush . . . O . . .

JOANNE N. LINMON. That's not a name.

SARAH R. It's going on. O.

JOANNE Mary Linmon Ro. Marilyn Monroe?

SARAH That's not how it's spelt.

DAWN Can people spell when they're dead?

JOANNE I should think they could spell their own names. It can't be Marilyn Monroe.

JULIE You were pushing it! It was Gas pushing it and being silly!

GAS No, it wasn't! I never pushed it. It moved itself.

JULIE I could feel somebody pushing it.

SARAH I don't want to do it if you're all being silly.

JOANNE It takes too long anyway, going round all the
letters.

JULIE We could do it the other way, you know, where
whatever it is knocks.

JOANNE Alright. Let's try that. Move the glass. Put the
candle back in the middle of the table. Now – all put
your hands on the table so everybody's hands are
touching.

JULIE Come on Gas, hands on table.

GAS Oh, do we have to?

JULIE Yes, we do. It's exciting. We'd have got an
answer then if you hadn't been silly.

JOANNE Somebody show Dawn how to put her hands.

SARAH Like this, Dawn.

JOANNE Are we all ready? Now, concentrate.
[*Dramatically*] Is there anybody there?

SARAH Quiet! It's no good if you don't concentrate.

JOANNE Is there anybody there?

> *There is a distant, hollow knock.* DAWN
> *whimpers.*

SARAH Did you hear that?

JOANNE That was somebody knocking.

DAWN What was it?

JULIE It was an answer. Ask it again.

JOANNE Is there anybody there?

> *They wait in silence. There is a second distant,*
> *hollow knock.* DAWN *whimpers again.*

JOANNE It knocked again.

SARAH It sounded a long way away, as though it was
upstairs.

JULIE Well, it's coming from beyond the grave.

DAWN Don't, don't!

JOANNE Keep your hands together. Don't move. It's
working. Are you trying to contact us?

> *They wait in silence. There is yet another
> distant, hollow knock.* DAWN *whimpers.*

JOANNE It's real. There *is* something.

SARAH What shall we ask it?

JULIE Ask it when I'm going to get married.

JOANNE Listen! I can hear footsteps.

SARAH There's a noise outside the door.

JULIE The door's opening!

> DAWN *is having quiet hysterics.*

SARAH It's Michael! Michael, you should be in bed.

MICHAEL I was in bed. I was asleep. And then there
was this noise.

JULIE He heard it as well!

MICHAEL Who's all these people? Is this who was
coming?

SARAH Yes. No. These are my friends. They just
happened to call on their way to somewhere else.

JOANNE Never mind that. What did you hear?

MICHAEL I heard a bang on the window. And I looked
out and it was a ghost.

SARAH There's no such things as ghosts.

MICHAEL And it was calling my name.

> DAWN *has more hysterics.*

JOANNE You can't see ghosts.
MICHAEL It was a face looking up and it had a white
 sheet round it.
JULIE That sounds like a ghost.
JOANNE You can't see ghosts.
DAWN Yes you can. I see my Gran's ghost nearly every
 night.

> *A silence but for* DAWN'S *whimpering.*

JOANNE Put the light on. Somebody put the light on.
SARAH I'll do it.
JOANNE Shut up, Dawn.

> *The light goes on.*

JOANNE That's better.
JULIE Where's Gas?
SARAH Don't cry, Dawn. It's alright now.
JULIE He's under the table. Gas is under the table!
GAS I dropped something.

> *There is a loud knock on the door. They all*
> *scream.*

JOANNE That's not a ghost. That's real. It's somebody
 at the door.
VOICE OFF Sarah! Sarah! It's Mrs Proctor.

SARAH It's Mrs Proctor from next door.

JOANNE Well, find out what she wants.

SARAH She'll see you all.

JOANNE Quick. All get under the table with Gas!

JULIE Under the table! This is fun! Come on, Dawn.

MICHAEL Shall I get under the table?

JOANNE No. You stay with us.

SARAH But don't you dare say anything.

JOANNE Go on then. Open it.

> SARAH *opens the door.* MRS PROCTOR *enters.*
> *She has a white towel over her head.*

SARAH Hello, Mrs Proctor.

PROCTOR Thank goodness. What a time I've had
making you hear. I couldn't see a light downstairs,
only one upstairs, so I've been throwing stones at the
bedroom window. Were you all in bed?

SARAH No. We were upstairs . . . putting Michael to
bed, that's all.

MICHAEL No, you weren't. I put myself to bed.

> SARAH *kicks him.*

PROCTOR There's a strong smell of beer . . . You don't
drink beer, do you? Anyway, what it is, is a message
from your mother. She's gone out without her key
and will you put one out for her under the mat. I've
had a terrible time making you hear. Do you
understand what I've just said? Put a key under the
mat.

SARAH Yes. I'll do that.

MICHAEL What have you got on your head, Mrs
Proctor?

PROCTOR This? It's an old towel, love. I threw it over
my head as I came out because it's raining a bit.
Good job I did, the time I've been out there. Are you
sure you're alright?

[SARAH *nods*.]

PROCTOR Well, I'll get back then. I'm missing *Dynasty*.
Now, you won't forget, will you?
SARAH No, Mrs Proctor. Thank you.

[MRS PROCTOR *goes*.]

SARAH Phew. I don't think she saw anything. But she
smelled that beer.
JOANNE So that was your ghost, Michael. I told you
you can't see ghosts.
MICHAEL Well, she looked like a ghost.

[JULIE, DAWN *and* GAS *crawl out from under the
table*.]

JULIE She looked an absolute scream in her towel. I
wish we had neighbours that dressed up.
DAWN I think I've lost my other ear-ring.
JULIE Well, that was ace, wasn't it, Gas?
SARAH I don't know whether I want to do any more
now . . .

[SARAH *blows out the candle*.]

JULIE Gas and I have got to go now anyway, haven't we Gas?

GAS [*Much relieved*] Yeah.

JULIE Are you coming, Dawn?

SARAH You can stay here, Dawn, if you like.

DAWN No. I'm going with them.

JULIE Right then. See you around. Bring the cider, Gas. That was really good.

> JULIE, GAS *and* DAWN *go.*

SARAH Bye, then.

JOANNE Goodbye.

SARAH Better clear up the mess. Help me lift this table back.

> *They tidy the room.*

MICHAEL Why have you got all these letters?

SARAH It was a game. My mum would ring up and spoil it all.

JOANNE Do you know what I think. I think it worked. I think what we were doing worked on your mum.

SARAH How do you mean?

JOANNE We were asking somebody to get in touch with us. And she did!

SARAH Could she do that?

MICHAEL Aren't you having this bag of crisps?

SARAH Yes we are. And you're going back to bed.

MICHAEL I'm frightened to go to bed after that ghost.

SARAH Come on then. You can stay up and share it with us.

THE PRESSURE-COOKER
STEVE SKIDMORE AND STEVE BARLOW

Characters

ANDREA

GRAHAM

DAWN

ANDREA'S MOTHER

IAN

Most human beings are capable of absorbing a lot of mental and emotional punishment. Sadly, some aren't. When someone attempts suicide, their reasons often seem trivial to an outside observer, who will be unaware that the immediate motive for a suicide attempt may be only the tip of an iceberg that has been building up for weeks, months or even years. We invited several students at our school to improvise a number of scenes showing the build up to such an attempt, and from their work scripted this play. It's their work as well as ours, and if it reads and sounds convincing, it is a tribute to their commitment and imagination that it does so.

Scene One

[*Outside school. Enter* GRAHAM *and* ANDREA.

ANDREA She'll kill me.

GRAHAM Who will?

ANDREA My mum.

GRAHAM Why?

ANDREA Don't you listen to me?

GRAHAM Not usually.

ANDREA Graham!

GRAHAM Only joking. Look, so you get bad results. It doesn't mean your mum's going to turn into Jack the Ripper and kill you.

ANDREA You don't know my mum.

GRAHAM [*Judge's voice*] Andrea Payne. You have been found guilty of obtaining low marks in your mock exams. I sentence you to be hung at dawn to set an example to other pupils who may . . .

ANDREA You're just not funny.

GRAHAM Sorry! Sorry I spoke. Sorry I breathe. Sorry I live.

ANDREA Shut up! I can't believe I did so badly.

GRAHAM Well, I'm rather pleased with my results.

ANDREA How did you get on?

GRAHAM Bottom in all of them! First time it's ever been done. A unique achievement, Jonesey said.

ANDREA You're stupid. I don't know why I bother with you.

GRAHAM Probably because of my stunning good looks, charm, wit, intelligence, and above all, my great modesty.

ANDREA Grow up, Graham.

GRAHAM You're in a right mood.

ANDREA Didn't think I'd do so badly.

GRAHAM What does it matter?

ANDREA A lot. What am I going to tell Mum?

GRAHAM Don't tell her.

ANDREA She knows I get the results today. What's she going to say?

GRAHAM I dunno. Mine won't say anything.

ANDREA Your mum's different to mine.

GRAHAM They're just mocks!

ANDREA I did badly in them. How am I going to do in the real ones?

GRAHAM Exams don't mean anything.

ANDREA Yes, they do! I want to go to drama college. What will I do if I fail them?

GRAHAM Do what I'm going to do – go on the dole.

ANDREA Oh, yes, you can have a really great time on the dole.

GRAHAM There's no jobs anyway, even if you've got exams.

ANDREA I don't believe how stupid you are sometimes.

Enter DAWN.

DAWN What's wrong with you two?

GRAHAM It's her. Worried about her results.

DAWN Well, they're only mocks.

ANDREA Don't you start. I suppose you did brilliantly.

DAWN I did OK. Anyway, I didn't revise for them.

GRAHAM Neither did I.

DAWN How did you do?

GRAHAM Came bottom in all of them!

ANDREA I did revise and I still did badly. Mum's going to murder me . . .

GRAHAM Here we go again.

DAWN You could do retakes in the sixth form.

ANDREA I can't. Mum says she can't afford to keep me on if I fail.

GRAHAM I thought your mum wanted you to go to
   university.

ANDREA She'll pay for me to do A levels. Not retakes.
   She reckons it's fair because my brother did A levels
   and went to university.

DAWN Mum and dad want *me* to go to university.

ANDREA Well, you're clever enough to get there.

GRAHAM I've not quite decided whether it's Oxford or
   Cambridge for me.

DAWN University?

GRAHAM No. Dole office!

DAWN Very funny.

ANDREA You really are stupid.

GRAHAM That's what Jonesey said. Bottom in every
   subject, Dawn. A unique achievement, he reckoned.

DAWN Well done! Anyway, I thought I'd remind you
   about my party on Saturday.

GRAHAM Great! I'm really looking forward to it.

ANDREA Who's going?

DAWN Everybody. Starts at eight o'clock. Mum and
   dad are going out, so it should be good. Bring a
   bottle.

GRAHAM Will milk do?

DAWN Ha ha! You ought to be on TV. Then we could
   switch you off. Are you coming, Andrea?

GRAHAM Of course she is.

ANDREA Yes, mum says I can go.

DAWN What are you two doing now?

GRAHAM Nothing.

DAWN D'you want to come round to my house and
   watch a video? Mum and dad are out.

ANDREA I can't. I've got to cook tea tonight. Mum's
   going to a meeting.

GRAHAM Stop worrying about your mum all the time.
   It's your life, not hers. Do what *you* want to do for a
   change.

DAWN Puts off telling her about the results.

ANDREA That's true.

GRAHAM Go on, live dangerously.

ANDREA Oh, alright.

DAWN Good.

GRAHAM About time too. Stop worrying about everything. Enjoy life.

ANDREA OK. Sorry. What's the video?

GRAHAM Zombie Zapping Vampire Flesh-Eaters? Or the Hacksaw Massacre?

DAWN Actually, it's Bambi. I thought you'd like it, Graham.

GRAHAM Ha ha, very funny. Come on, let's go.

Scene Two

> MOTHER *is getting ready to go out.* ANDREA *enters: she is surprised at seeing* MOTHER *still in.*

ANDREA Oh!

MOTHER So you've come home. What time do you call this?

ANDREA Sorry, Mum, I was at Dawn's watching a video.

MOTHER Watching a video! Never mind about getting tea ready; never mind your mother's got a meeting to go to. Andrea's at Dawn's watching a video. Very nice indeed. Well, thank you Andrea.

ANDREA I said I was sorry.

MOTHER Honestly, Andrea, it's not fair. I work all day so that you can have a decent home. I get no help from you. You do nothing in the home. Not a thing.

ANDREA That's not true.

MOTHER When was the last time you hoovered or dusted? God knows it's hard enough without your father. I thought you might help out a bit.

ANDREA I do. You know I do.

MOTHER Well, maybe you could do a bit more. For instance, you could cook the meal when you know I've got a meeting to go to.

ANDREA Alright, Mum, don't go on.

MOTHER 'Don't go on!' That's a fine thing to say: 'Don't go on'. Thank you, Andrea. Anyway, because you weren't here, I had to cook the meal. There's some meat in the oven and potatoes and carrots in the pressure-cooker.

ANDREA You know I don't like spuds out of the pressure-cooker. They go all soggy.

MOTHER Perhaps you should have thought of that when you were watching the video. I had to use the pressure-cooker because I'm in a rush. So you'll have to like it. And don't try to take the lid off before it stops hissing. You're lucky to get anything at all.

ANDREA Sorry.

MOTHER I should think so . . . Pass my lipstick, will you, it's on the side.

ANDREA Here.

MOTHER Thank you – oh yes, another thing; you were getting your results today. How did you get on?

ANDREA [*Quietly*] OK.

MOTHER Oh, Andrea, you've not let me down have you?

ANDREA Did my best.

MOTHER What do you mean, you did your best? How bad were they?

ANDREA Bad.

MOTHER How bad is 'bad'?

ANDREA Very bad.

MOTHER Andrea! I give up with you. How much revision did you do?

ANDREA Loads. You know I stayed in and worked.

MOTHER You obviously didn't work hard enough. How did the others do? How did Dawn do? I bet she did well, didn't she? I bet she did a lot of revision.

ANDREA Didn't do any.

MOTHER But I'm sure she got good marks, didn't she? Andrea, you've got to work harder. If you don't, you'll never get to university.

ANDREA I don't want to go to university. I want to go to drama college.

MOTHER Don't be stupid, Andrea. We've talked about this. Just because you're in the school play you think you're going to be a great actress.

ANDREA I want to go to drama college!

MOTHER I'm not discussing this any more. We've decided that you're going to university.

ANDREA *You've* decided.

MOTHER I want you to do well for yourself. Like Ian.

ANDREA It's always Ian, isn't it? Ian this. Ian that. Isn't Ian wonderful?

MOTHER Don't be so cheeky.

ANDREA You want me to be Ian.

MOTHER No I don't. Don't be so silly.

ANDREA I'm not Ian, I'm me. I want to do what I want to do, not what everyone else wants me to do. It's my life.

MOTHER That's right. And I want the best for you. I want you to go to university and get a decent job and do well. I want what's best for you.

ANDREA What's best for me is what I want to do.

MOTHER Getting bad results?

ANDREA I didn't mean to get bad results.

MOTHER You didn't mean to get good ones either. If you had, you'd have spent more time revising instead of seeing *him*.

ANDREA Who?

MOTHER You know who I mean. You see far too much of that boy.

ANDREA He's got a name, mum. He's called Graham.

MOTHER Yes, that's him. Graham. I don't know what you see in him. Honestly, I don't. How did *he* get on in the exams?

ANDREA What's it matter how he got on.

MOTHER I see, as badly as you, I imagine. I've told you, Andrea, I'm not letting you stay on to do retakes.

ANDREA Mum, I worked as hard as I could, honestly.

MOTHER You still went out though.

ANDREA I can't stay in all the time.

MOTHER It wouldn't hurt! Perhaps if you had, you might have got better results. Ian never went out, and he got good results.

ANDREA Ian again. Ian. Little favourite Ian. Goody-goody Ian. [*Mimics mother*] Oh, Ian's so clever. Andrea's so thick. My son Ian, he's at university. I love Ian so much. He's a lovely boy. Is that why Dad left? Because you loved Ian so much?

MOTHER *slaps* ANDREA's *face.* ANDREA *starts to cry.*

MOTHER Don't you ever talk to me like that. It was because of you that he left – not Ian. You. Left me to bring up both of you. And I will. And you'll get good

qualifications and good jobs. I'll make sure you do.
If you can't help yourself, then I'll have to do it for
you. Understand? First of all, you're staying in. No
more going out until the exams are over.

ANDREA You can't make me.

MOTHER Can't I? Just you see. For a start, you're not
going to that party tomorrow.

ANDREA You said I could!

MOTHER Well, after tonight, I've changed my mind.

ANDREA But I've told Graham I'm going.

MOTHER That's another thing – no more seeing him.
You've got work to do.

ANDREA That's not fair.

MOTHER I don't care what's fair, Andrea. You're
staying in, and that's that.

ANDREA I hate you.

MOTHER You'll thank me in the long run.

ANDREA [*Running out and slamming the door*] No I
won't. I hate you.

Scene Three

> *Outside school.* GRAHAM *is propping a wall up.*
> ANDREA *enters looking sheepish. He affects not
> to notice her.*

ANDREA Hiya.

GRAHAM Oh, hello.

ANDREA Sorry.

GRAHAM Sorry? What for?

ANDREA The party.

GRAHAM What about it?

ANDREA Not going.

GRAHAM   Oh, you was going to go, was you?

ANDREA   Oh, come off it.

GRAHAM   Off what?

ANDREA   [*With determined patience*] I'm sorry I
couldn't go to the party with you.

GRAHAM   Couldn't?

ANDREA   That's right, couldn't. Mum wouldn't let me
out.

GRAHAM   Oh, well, that's OK. We had a great time.

ANDREA   Oh yes?

GRAHAM   Yeah, really great party. Pity you *couldn't*
go.

ANDREA   I couldn't!

GRAHAM   You said.

ANDREA   You don't understand.

GRAHAM   Right.

ANDREA   I really wanted to go.

GRAHAM   So why didn't you?

ANDREA   I told you. Mum wouldn't let me.

GRAHAM   Oh? What did she do, then? Tie you to a
chair? Lock you in your room and swallow the key?
Make you take a bath and then wash all the towels?

ANDREA   She says I'm seeing too much of you.

GRAHAM   Oh, she does?

ANDREA   She says I've got to stop going out in the
evenings. Got to stay in. Study.

GRAHAM   And what do you say?

ANDREA   I've got to get my exams . . .

GRAHAM   So you're giving in. As usual. [*Puts on
Master of Ceremony voice*] Ladeez an' Gennelmun,
we proudly present – the world's leading
ventriloquist, Councillor Payne, with Andrea!
[*Snooty female voice*] 'Now, Andrea, I want you to
stop seeing Graham.' [*As doll*] 'Googye, Graygam.'

ANDREA   Don't be like that.

GRAHAM How d'you expect me to be?

ANDREA We don't have to stop seeing each other. I mean, we can still walk to school together. And back.

GRAHAM Yeah, great relationship. Could talk a lot then, couldn't we?

ANDREA You're not talking to me now.

GRAHAM 'Course I'm talking to you now – what d'you think this is?

ANDREA You know I'd've come if I could.

GRAHAM No, it's not your mum at all. It's you. You don't want to see me anymore – but that's alright, Andrea.

ANDREA It's not that!

GRAHAM Yes it is. Getting dead snobby, you are. All this about going to drama college. What d'you want to go there for? Doing stupid plays with a bunch of woofters. Won't be good enough for you then, will I? Just 'cos I'm not going to college, you think I'm nothing.

ANDREA That's not what I think.

GRAHAM It's what your mum thinks, isn't it? So it's what you think.

ANDREA That's not true.

GRAHAM Isn't it? You could still go out with me, couldn't you? You wouldn't have to tell your mum.

ANDREA What if she found out, though?

GRAHAM What if she did?

ANDREA She said, if I didn't stop seeing you, she'd stop me going to drama college.

GRAHAM [*Sarcastic*] Oh, well, that's alright, then.

ANDREA Look, I really love you – I've told you before.

GRAHAM You really show it, don't you?

ANDREA I do!

GRAHAM   Just not enough. Why don't you fight her for once?

ANDREA   I can't. I'm not that strong. She overpowers me all the time.

GRAHAM   You let her.

ANDREA   Graham . . .

GRAHAM   What?

ANDREA   Nothing.

[*Pause.*]

ANDREA   Good, was it then? This party?

GRAHAM   Yeah, we had a great time.

ANDREA   We?

GRAHAM   Yeah, well, everybody.

ANDREA   Dance with anybody?

GRAHAM   A few.

ANDREA   Who?

GRAHAM   Just girls.

ANDREA   I guessed that. Who?

GRAHAM   Well, if you'd been there, you'd know, wouldn't you?

ANDREA   Why don't you want to tell me?

GRAHAM   Isn't that the bell?

ANDREA   Graham?

GRAHAM   [*Snapping*] Look – I went there on my own, right? You know I hate going places like that on my own.

ANDREA   She wouldn't let me out!

GRAHAM   You didn't even phone to say you weren't coming.

ANDREA   You knew when I wasn't there, I wasn't coming. You knew my mum'd kill me for my exam results.

[*Dawn comes by.*]

DAWN Hi, Graham. Hello Andrea. Come on, you'll be late for registration.

GRAHAM Coming.

DAWN See you tonight, then, Graham.

[*She goes.* GRAHAM *looks and sounds sheepish.*]

ANDREA What's going on?

GRAHAM How d'you mean?

ANDREA Dawn. You. With Dawn. At the party. My best mate.

GRAHAM So what if I was? Can't blame me, can you?

ANDREA Yes I can. You just don't care, do you?

GRAHAM In a way, yeah.

ANDREA In a way?

GRAHAM I thought about you a bit.

ANDREA A bit? Oh, thanks, Graham.

GRAHAM Yeah, a bit. On the way there, I thought, 'I wonder how Andrea's doing.'

ANDREA I thought about you all night. All the time. Couldn't do my work. Couldn't do anything. Thinking about you. And there you were. You and Dawn. Brilliant mates I've got.

GRAHAM So whose fault's that? Always somebody else's fault, isn't it? Me, your mum, Dawn. Not you. Never you.

ANDREA Don't.

GRAHAM Try thinking about someone else for a change. [*She goes*] Miss I Am. Me, me, me. I love me, who do you love? Who do you love, Andrea? Who loves ya, baby?

ANDREA [*From a distance*] Nobody.

Scene Four

> *School: The fifth form room. Several pupils are*
> *chatting.* ANDREA *is reading a magazine.* DAWN
> *and* GRAHAM *come in.*

GRAHAM [*Snatching magazine*] Studying again?

ANDREA Hey! That magazine's mine! Give it back!

GRAHAM Ought to be ashamed of yourself. What
would Mummy say? What's this? *Teentalk*. Very
intellectual.

DAWN Ooh, don't you know some big words.

GRAHAM Watch it. Here, look, she's only reading the
problem page, isn't she?

DAWN Oh, Andrea.

ANDREA What's it got to do with you? It's my
magazine – I can read any page I want. Give it here.

DAWN Oh, sorry I spoke.

ANDREA Give it back, Graham, please.

GRAHAM Hang on a minute, good for a laugh these
letters are. Here's one – listen to this: 'Dear
Emily . . .'

DAWN Emily?

GRAHAM That's her name: 'Teentalk helpline – having
problems with boys, your work, your parents or
your body? Write to me, Emily. . . .'

DAWN Emily!

GRAHAM Shut up and listen. 'Dear Emily, I've got a
boy-friend and I really like him, but he keeps asking
me to go to bed with him. I don't want to because I
want to be a virgin when I get married, and anyway,
it gives me a headache . . .'

DAWN Stupid! You made that up.

GRAHAM They're all made up, aren't they? No one'd

really write a letter like that to go in a magazine where everyone'd see it.

DAWN Nobody *did* write a letter like that.

GRAHAM Alright, I'll read one out of here – oh, here's a good 'un.

ANDREA No!

GRAHAM 'Dear Emily, I'm only thirteen, but I have very big breasts for my age. [*All the others in the room react: oooh!*] My mum's very strict and she says I can't have a bra because I'm too young, but they keep moving about under my pullover.
[*Laughter and lewd comments*] The boys in our class keep looking at me, and the girls say I'm showing off. What can I do?

DAWN I bet you made that up as well.

GRAHAM I never – it's here, look. You're not telling me someone'd really write that in to a magazine.

DAWN People do.

GRAHAM Come off it.

DAWN Some of the advice they give is really helpful.

GRAHAM Could do better myself.

DAWN Oh yes? Give it here, then. Let's try you out.

ANDREA Stop it. I want my magazine back.

DAWN Just a minute. Right. 'Dear Aunt Emily . . .'

GRAHAM [*Auntie voice*] Yes?

DAWN 'When I was at junior school, I got worms.
[*Reaction: uuurgh!*] When I started secondary school, I got them again, and my mum was furious and said if I got them again, I'd have to go into hospital and have an operation. Now I *have* got them again, and I daren't tell my mum. I always wash my hands when I've been to the loo, so it's not my fault. Worried *Teentalk* reader.'

GRAHAM [*Auntie voice*] 'Dear Worried *Teentalk* reader, the answer to your problem is very simple.

After you've been to the loo, you must wash your hands *before* you bite your fingernails.' [*Others laugh*]

DAWN Oh, very funny.

GRAHAM Come on, then, I'll do one for you. Here we are – the Star Letter, from 'Desperate reader'. 'Dear Auntie Emily . . .'

ANDREA Graham! Stop it! Give it back! *Give it back*!

> *She struggles to get the magazine.* DAWN *holds her.*

GRAHAM Hey up, hang on to her. She's going mad. Here we go: 'Dear Auntie Emily, I'm writing to you because I don't know what else to do . . .'

ANDREA No! Give it to me! It's mine!

GRAHAM Oh, don't be so mardy . . . 'I haven't got a dad, only a mum, and I can't talk to her, she's always out at meetings.' Cor, real tear-jerker this, isn't it?

ANDREA Stop it. Please. Please stop it, Graham.

GRAHAM 'Anyway, she doesn't listen. She wants me to go to university. We keep having rows about it. I want to go to drama college, but I've mucked up all my exams . . .' Hey, this could be you, Andrea. 'On top of that, she's told me to stop seeing my boyfriend.'

DAWN Graham, pack it in.

GRAHAM Just a minute, nearly finished. 'I really love him, but he's started going out with my best mate . . .' [*At last, he has become aware of the silence: uncertainly*] Here, what's up?

ANDREA You pig. You filthy rotten dirty pig.

> *She takes the magazine and goes.*

GRAHAM What's got into her?

DAWN You can be really thick sometimes, can't you?

GRAHAM You what?

DAWN You even said it yourself.

GRAHAM You mean – she did write that letter? Andrea?

DAWN Congratulations!

GRAHAM I never thought . . .

DAWN You never do. You've really upset her now.

GRAHAM Me? What about you? Best mate.

DAWN You asked me out.

GRAHAM You didn't exactly fight me off, did you?

DAWN You shouldn't have read that letter out.

GRAHAM How was I supposed to know?

DAWN You shouldn't have teased her.

GRAHAM Oh, I might've known it was all my fault.

DAWN I wonder if she's alright.

GRAHAM She's alright.

DAWN I should go round and see her tonight . . .

GRAHAM What about the film?

DAWN We can go another time.

GRAHAM Finishes tonight.

DAWN I suppose I could go round tomorrow. Or the day after. Don't know why I should feel guilty, anyway – I didn't make her fail her rotten exams. Bet she wouldn't want to see me if I did go.

GRAHAM See you after school then.

DAWN Yeah, see you. Poor Andrea. The look on her face. Bit of a laugh, though, wasn't it?

Scene Five

> *Outside* ANDREA's *house.* DAWN *rings the doorbell.* IAN *answers.*

DAWN Oh, hello. Is Andrea in?

IAN No.

DAWN Oh.Um – you're Ian, aren't you? Andrea's brother?

IAN That's right. Are you a friend of Andrea's?

DAWN Yes – at least – we had a bit of a row . . . she hasn't been at school for a day or two. I wondered . . .

IAN Are you Dawn?

DAWN Yes.

IAN You'd better come in. Through here – in the kitchen. I'm just cooking supper. Don't want to leave it.

> *The pressure-cooker is whistling.*

DAWN What's that noise?

IAN Pressure-cooker. I'm doing the spuds. The safety-valve's letting off a bit of steam. I'll turn the heat down: it'll stop in a minute.

DAWN Makes a racket, doesn't it?

IAN You've got to have a safety-valve on a pressure-cooker. Could blow up if you didn't.

DAWN Will Andrea be home soon?

IAN No.

DAWN Well, I could come back tomorrow.

IAN How'd she been? These last few days?

DAWN Well . . .

IAN Bit upset would you say?

DAWN A bit, yeah.

IAN Any idea what about?

DAWN Well, exams. And she was worried her mum might not let her go to drama college.

IAN And?

DAWN We had a bit of a row, like. About a boy. I wanted to make it up.

IAN That all?

DAWN Well, there was this letter. In a magazine.

IAN I found the magazine.

DAWN We was laughing about it. At school. Didn't know it was her. She was upset. A bit.

IAN A bit. Just a bit. Only a bit.

DAWN Look, can I see Andrea?

IAN Andrea's in hospital.

DAWN What?

IAN That's why I'm here. Mum called me at university.

DAWN But – what? – I mean – was it an accident?

IAN Not an accident. She swallowed mum's sleeping pills. Nearly a whole bottle. Mum was out.

DAWN Oh my God . . . I never thought . . . not Andrea. Why?

IAN Don't you know?

DAWN I can't believe it.

IAN You can go and see her – she's all wired up like Frankenstein's monster – tubes going in, tubes coming out, in her arms, down her throat.

DAWN I'll go and see her – or is your mum . . .?

IAN Mum's at a meeting.

DAWN At a *meeting*? Not at the hospital?

IAN There's no point. Andrea's in a coma. Know what that means?

DAWN 'Course I know what it means. Don't the doctors know when she'll wake up?

IAN The doctors don't know *if* she'll wake up. They said they'd ring if anything happened.

DAWN Oh, God, it's my fault. Poor Andrea.

IAN Bit late to be sorry, isn't it?

DAWN What d'you mean?

IAN Pity you weren't sorrier a bit earlier – you and this Graham.

DAWN How d'you know about . . . how did you know who I was?

IAN She mentioned your names. In the note.

DAWN Note?

IAN They always leave a note. [*Pause*] There, see, it's stopped.

DAWN What?

IAN The noise from the steam. That means the pressure's back to normal. Unless the safety-valve's got blocked. I've heard of that happening. Then you could be in dead trouble. You can't always tell, can you?

[
In another part of the house, the telephone starts to ring.
]

THE WEEPING MADONNA
PETER TERSON

Characters

MELANIE, a girl who buys the MADONNA

MUM

GRANDPA

NEIGHBOURS

REPORTER

CROWDS OF BELIEVERS

CROWDS OF DOUBTERS

CHIEF CONSTABLE

COUNCIL OFFICIALS

DOCTOR

POLITICIAN

PRIEST

PLUMBER

PSYCHOLOGIST

METEOROLOGIST

People often ask playwrights, 'How long does it take you to write a play?'

The Weeping Madonna is a good example to use in reply.

It took me two morning sessions to write (about ninety minutes each session), but the idea had been churning round in my head for thirty two years!

Yes, honestly.

The phenomenon of the real Weeping Madonna occurred in Newcastle upon Tyne in 1955 and was reported in the local papers.

I was a young teacher at the time, when a girl in Walker saw tears coming from the eyes of her plaster cast.

I went down and saw the bedlam outside her house: the hysteria, the hope, the jeering, the doubting, the curiosity and general uproar.

For many years the idea kept emerging in my mind, trying to form itself into a play, but only now has the Weeping Madonna come to life.

Perhaps that's my little miracle.

NARRATOR Note you all, who at your school desks sit,
And in the schoolroom chafe.
A domestic interior, a table, chairs, to set the scene.
No doubt it is common enough, the sort where most
    of you have been.
So, stay awake, alert, kindle the imagination
And I will vouchsafe to move you,
If not to tears and laughter,
Then at least to thought.
Or else add a new dimension to subjects taught.

A mother waits and worries, as mothers do.
What is on her mind? How can it be told?
Just wait, and see
And it will all unfold.

> *Enter* GRANDPA.

MUM She isn't back yet.
GRANDPA Who?
MUM You know who.

GRANDPA It isn't late.

MUM She said she'd be back.

GRANDPA Where has she gone?

MUM I don't know, that's the trouble.

GRANDPA You can't keep them on a line all their life.

MUM I know but since her father's gone . . .

GRANDPA Him, I want to hear none of him.

NARRATOR Tension in the air, I do declare.
　　But a glimpse through any window
　　Behind any curtain, will show a family drama
　　That's for certain.

[　*Enter daughter,* MELANIE.　]

　　Enter daughter,
　　With something in parcel wrap't.
　　What can it be?
　　Has mother noticed?
　　Will she mention it?
　　Or ignore it?
　　Blunder in. . . . use discretion?
　　Exercise tact?

GRANDPA Hello love.

MELANIE Hello Grandpa.

MUM Where have you been dear? Not that it's any of
　　my business if you don't want to tell me.

MELANIE To market.

MUM Which market?

LUCY Just the market.

MUM Indoor market? Or outdoor market?

LUCY That's right. That market.

MUM I didn't know you needed anything. At market.

LUCY I didn't need anything.

MUM So you got nothing.

LUCY I got something.

MUM But you didn't need it?

LUCY I might have need of it.

GRANDPA Now there's a riddle, hey diddle diddle,
  I do like a riddle.
  You had need of nothing.
  But you got something,
  And might find need of the thing,
  It could be anything.
  Is it a plaything?

MUM That's enough Grandpa, you're wandering.

MELANIE *unwraps the parcel and brings out a garish Virgin Mary.*

MUM My God, what's that?

MELANIE It's a Madonna.

MUM How did you come by that?

MELANIE It was like this . . . quite strange really,
  I was wandering round the market,
  Going from stall to stall,
  With nothing there for me at all.
  When down dropped the side of a van
  And up popped a roving salesman.
  And banging on a box to gain attention, said
  'Gather round you lucky folks,
  You're in for a bargain,
  To give stuff away is my intention.'

GRANDPA A mock auctioneer!
  Tricksters, phoneys, the lot of 'em.
  Diddle you out of your savings and pension.

MELANIE 'I have for you a selection of works of Art'

He told the crowd that quickly gathered.
'I'm not asking full price, nor half, not a quarter of
   its full value.
Come along, if you're good to me I'll play my part.'
In this way he sold plaster casts of elephants,
With tusks,
Of fierce-eyed Arabs, with hawked features,
Of Indians, Gypsies, exotic animals and creatures.
Then he brought out this. There was a hush.
'What am I offered for this little lush?'
But no offers came.

MUM I'm not surprised, people don't go to mock
auctioneers for their religious objects.

MELANIE 'It's only one off,' he cried, 'A Virgin Mary.'
I shan't ask full price, not half, not quarter,
I'll crucify myself more than I oughta . . .
Who'll take it for a TENTH of its value
Before I put it back, to your disgrace,
Into its straw in the packing case.'
I looked at her face, and seemed to hear a voice,
quite still, among the din
say, 'Melanie, take me in.'
And quite contrary to my intention,
Put up my hand and accepted the bargain.

MOTHER How much?

MELANIE A tenth of its value.

MOTHER How much?

MELANIE In the shops they're £25.

MOTHER How much?

MELANIE Three pound.

GRANDPA Three pound; that's not a tenth of twenty-
five.
Blokes like that should be skinned alive.

MOTHER Three pounds, what a waste.
And not to my taste.

MELANIE I like her.

MOTHER It's not a 'HER' it's an 'IT'.

And I don't like her one little bit.

NARRATOR And so the plaque was put up on Melanie's wall.

Though Mum was dubious, in fact she didn't like the idea at all.

However she had the neighbours in, as mothers do,

When they're troubled in their mind

And not sure what to do . . .

> *Enter neighbours,* MRS AUSTIN *and* MRS FORD.

MUM There it is . . . it makes me uneasy . . .

AUSTIN I must say it's a bit thick.

FORD You're not Roman Catholic?

MUM Not at all . . . not since I've been married have I been to Church,

And a lot of good that did me when he left me in the lurch.

AUSTIN Well it's alright, I suppose. A Virgin Mary.

MUM It makes the place like a seminary.

I'm uneasy; there's something I don't like, you see,

About mystic behaviour in our Melanie . . .

AUSTIN It might be, you know, her time of life.

FORD It's such a worrying time with girls.

AUSTIN Emotional problems take many forms this age.

FORD If they don't run off with Hells Angels

They want to go up on the stage.

AUSTIN It's harmless, queer but harmless,

Consider the money well spent.

FORD If the worst comes to the worst you can stick her in a Convent.

[*They go.*]

NARRATOR Now we come to the drama . . .
One morning Melanie looked up at her sweet-faced
    cast,
  And saw UNMISTAKABLY CLEAR . . .
  The first tear . . .

[MELANIE *goes down on her knees.*]

MUM'S VOICE Melanie, Melanie, are you alright?
  You're very quiet, are you reading by the light?

[*Enter* MUM.]

What's this? On your knees?
Oh God, don't give her religion . . .
What a disease . . .

[GRANDPA *enters.*]

GRANDPA What's this? Oh God, a bout of prayer.
  Have we had the Mormons? Plymouth Brethren?
  Born again Christians?
  They're everywhere . . .
MUM I hope you're not getting religion.
  Life's hard enough with survival,
  Let alone a revival.

[MELANIE *points.*]

MELANIE Look . . . see for yourself . . . a tear . . .

MUM Where?

MELANIE There.

GRANDPA Has anybody seen my spec case, I leave the
damned thing everywhere . . .

MELANIE See, she weeps.

MUM This can't be true.

GRANDPA It must be, and if they're tears I'll tell you
what we'll do.

Lick 'em, if they're salty it must be true.

MELANIE Grandpa, don't . . . I don't want PROOF.

I just want faith under this roof.

Perhaps she's trying to TELL US SOMETHING.

Perhaps she has a message to convey,

And she'll impart it to us, this way.

Perhaps she weeps for the state of man,

And would like him to change while he can.

Or else they are tears of despair.

That we commit such horrors everywhere.

Or are they tears of hope?

And she comes to show us an open door

To a new, and happy life beyond our knowledge.

GRANDPA That sort of message comes out of books at
College.

MELANIE Perhaps she's trying to tell us in a simple
way.

MUM Yes, well, one thing, let's keep it quiet till it goes
away.

GRANDPA Aye, or we'll have snoopers round, then
we'll rue the day . . .

NARRATOR But word got round, and how do you keep
the neighbours out

When there's something out of the ordinary
about . . .

AUSTIN On her knees, your Melanie . . .
    Have you had the doctor in?

MUM No, I thought I'd wait and see.

FORD They look like tears, and don't they run quite
    freely.

MUM They vary, come and go, sometimes damp the
    carpet nearly.

AUSTIN I've heard of miracles on the telly,
    Miracle soap powders, miracle machines,
    Miracle labour-saving devices,
    But nothing like this, you should take advice.

FORD I know a man who goes to Lourdes every year
    for a miracle cure,
    He's a cripple, but got plenty of money,
    It's not for the poor.

AUSTIN Does it do him any good, going on these
    pilgrimages?

FORD He's still in a wheelchair, but he's had it for
    ages.

MOTHER Well, there, you know our secret, I've got it
    off my chest.
    You won't tell anybody, will you? I think that's best.

AUSTIN Oh, you know us, not a word.

FORD It will be as secret with us as if we'd never
    heard . . .

NARRATOR And so the news was spread from mouth to
    mouth,
    But no one would confess how it got out,
    In shops, laundrettes, bus-stops and public places.
    Blathering tongues and eager faces.
    'There's a miracle in our neighbourhood.'
    The truth was out, for bad or good,
    Then in came the local reporter with his pencil and
    pad . . .

Enter REPORTER.

REPORTER I'll get this into the Nationals and Dailies as
    a front page spread.
MUM Don't let's have any publicity, it's one thing I
    dread.
REPORTER You can't keep a miracle ALL TO
    YOURSELF.
    You must share the Weeping Madonna . . .
    She might be a virgin, but she can't be hid on the
    shelf . . .
NARRATOR And so they came from miles around.
    With television cameras, light and sound.
    And as the story was told, and retold,
    Still the tears down the Virgin's cheeks rolled.
    And the news went round the land like fire,
    Until there were crowds, queues, a silver band and a
    choir . . .

    People came from miles around to stare and try to
    touch,
    And see the girl on her knees who was moved so
    much.
VISITORS Eeeh, it's a sign from God.
    She's warning us about something.
    It looks like a tear, it seems like a tear.
    She's weeping for us.
    Sin no more, the end of the world is at hand.
    She despairs for the world.
    We've brought it on ourselves.
NARRATOR Everybody tried to stake a claim,
    On the Madonna and her Fame.
    Even the Church came to stare.
    And once convinced they claimed their share.

PRIEST This is not a religious neighbourhood, I must admit,

My Church has been under-attended for some years, but I submit,

That this will bring in more than a few,

To fill up the empty pew,

So, 'Whatever your creed, or belief, or denomination,

Praise this sign from the God of all Creation.'

NARRATOR The Council Officials came to make her fit,

Their book of rules and licences, to wit . . .

OFFICIAL 1 Under what clause can we tax her?

Is she a rateable, or taxable factor?

OFFICIAL 2 There must be a document in our files and forms

To license this above the norm.

BOTH We are Council Officials; we like things taxed and taped,

Licences and approvals and consents

Are the stuff of what we're made . . .

OFFICIAL 1 We have a file personae on every living soul on our Council List,

OFFICIAL 2 But a WEEPING MADONNA we seem to have overlooked and missed.

But despite public opinion or emotional pressure we'll not be denied.

We'll have this miracle classified.

NARRATOR Politicians came to do the same.

Claim her for right and left, the same old game.

All came until the Mighty rabble,

Corrupted the sanctity with their babble.

There were advertisers,

Publicists, film-makers

Cheeky kids and miracle fakers.

Profiteers, racketeers.
Invalids who prayed to walk.
Folk who did nothing but talk talk talk
Doubters, and shouters.
Deniers, defiers.
The faithful few,
Those to themselves who were true.
The needy, the worried,
The loiterers, the hurried.
The calm, the thoughtful and the pensive.
The wild, the skinheads and the offensive . . .
ALL . . . ALL . . . fought to get a glimpse of HER at
    last,
The MOTHER of GOD, or a plaster cast.
Out in the streets spilled the action,
There were claims and denial of every faction,
There were fights, riots and love-ins and hysteria,
But the solution of the mystery came no nearer.
People fought and struggled into the dark.
And open air services were held in the park.
Seers, prophets and witches came out of their lairs,
Where they'd been waiting for hundreds of years.
A State of Emergency was being demanded.
Until the Police came in heavy handed . . .

CHIEF CONSTABLE STOP! this is causing CIVIL
    DISTURBANCE that won't be allowed.
You are behaving illegally, as individuals
And as a crowd.

NARRATOR With that he gathered round him the men
    of power and position,
To test their feelings and disposition.

CONSTABLE This position is getting out of hand,
Any mob we must disperse and disband . . .
Now, one by one, state your cases, and be wary,

Because I'll make my report to the Home Secretary.

COUNCIL OFFICIAL As a Council Official I protest at the use of Council Property.

Being used like a peep show, or OFFERTORY . . .

DOCTOR As a doctor I fear the effects of mass hysteria on those easily led.

And bona fide invalids getting up from their National Health beds.

POLITICIAN As a politician I am afraid this is being used by unscrupulous factions

To bring about change and revolutionary actions.

PRIEST As a priest I now see I was wrong in my assessment.

People now want miracles, not an ordained priest in his vestment.

CONSTABLE Right, we are agreed this must be put a stop to.

ALL Agreed.

POLITICIAN But not by force, you must do it with tact . . .

Or else the people might violently react . . .

COUNCIL OFFICIAL We must do it by persuasion . . .

Spread doubt and scorn, reveal it as a fake.

This is the best, and only course we can take.

CHIEF CONSTABLE Then on the course we're all agreed,

Each of you will provide an expert in your field,

See what dividend this will yield.

NARRATOR And so, council, doctor, politician, priest briefed a so-called 'expert' specialist

To cast the seed of doubt and cast their damning opinion on it . . .

[

Enter BOROUGH ENGINEER.

]

BOROUGH ENGINEER I am the Borough Engineer of
Water, Heat and Ventilation,
  And in my experience I've seen examples of this little
complication.
  It's all to do with thermo-internal condensation
  That creeps through walls, finds a porous patch
  And results in this evaporation.

>   *Enter* BISHOP.

BISHOP I am the Bishop of the High Church and come
    to this Diocese,
  To find all these people on their knees.
  God himself has told us not to look for miracles,
  But to FAITH hold true.
  This is an example of mass hallucination
  Induced by the devil to corrupt you.

>   *Enter* PSYCHOLOGIST.

PSYCHOLOGIST As a psychologist I can inform you that
    it has been known,
  For people, even children, to FORCE a supernatural
    phenomenon of their own.
  Through sheer will power, and focus of their cranial
    matter,
  They have been known to bend nails, levitate, and
    even glass to shatter.

>   *Enter* METEOROLOGIST.

METEOROLOGIST I'm a meteorologist, I study the
weather, humidity and cloud formation.
And I can understand why this appearance of
moisture receives your approbation.
But in fact the explanation is quite clear,
It's the result of moisture in the atmosphere,
Meeting isobars, troughs, low pressure and upward-
rising condensation,
I've had reports of this climatic freak coming in to
my weather station.

POLITICIAN I am in the Diplomatic Service, secret, hush
hush.
And believe me, you are being manipulated.
These tears have been technologically induced
By a foreign power to bring down your
Government who've been mandated.

CHIEF CONSTABLE In other words it's got a logical
explanation,
Now, move along and relieve this congestion.
The thing has been revealed for what it is at last.
Not a Weeping Madonna, but a flawed plaster cast.

COUNCIL OFFICIAL I am a Council Official and though I
hate to mention,
This is a trick, a ploy to gain sympathy.
Her mother has applied for a rent rebate
And an indexed pension.

VOICES It's a fake.
Swindle.
It's a sign from God.
Twist. Cheat.
Hallelujah, the end of the world is nigh.

VOICES Let's have a riot.
Tear her down. Break the place up.
Protestants. Catholics. Schemers.
Off your knees.

Tear her down. Break the place up.
We shall not, we shall not be moved.
Lord, a sign, show us your wrath . . . a sign.
I'll have it, it's mine.
It's too sacred to touch . . .
MELANIE [*rising*] Stop.

[*Takes down the cast. It weeps on her hand.*]

I bought this cast as a simple act.
And for the first time in my life I felt something
     beyond dull fact.
I felt a bond, a warmth, a meaning, a universal
     philosophy
But you've brought greed, mania, doubt and
     mockery.
Your eyes blurred with your self-induced hysteria,
Have seen the truth no clearer.
Whether she cries or not, I only know
She brought peace into my life,
Now she must go.

[*Smashes the cast to smithereens.*]

PLAYWRIGHTS

Peter Terson

When I was doing a course in Writing for Sixth Formers with the Arden Foundation, a girl came up to me and asked, 'Are you Peter Terson?'

'Yes,' I replied.

She looked at me with wonder and said, 'I thought you must be dead.'

Well I'm not dead, but looking back my early life seems another existence.

I was born in 1932, the son of a joiner and last child of a mother worn out with 'work and worry'. The two 'W's of that period.

I was brought up on bread and dripping and passed the Entrance Exam for Heaton Grammar School, so much to my father's amazement that he told me to ring up the Education Office to see if they'd made a mistake.

However, I'd passed, but finishing with an undistinguished record have always feared my father may have been right.

I then had three consecutive failures, as a draughtsman, as an airman and as a teacher, then I sent a play to the Victoria Theatre, Stoke on Trent and the Director, Peter Cheeseman, nominated me as Resident Playwright and the Arts Council gave me a year's salary of £900. While I was there Michael Croft of the National Youth Theatre asked me to write a play for 'about a hundred kids' and I wrote him *Zigger Zagger*.

They were my glorious days, but I'm not dead yet and just coming up to my peak (confidence and mad optimism is all to the playwright).

Arnold Wesker

Arnold Wesker was born in London in 1932. He has written over twenty plays for the stage, in addition to scripts for TV, radio and film and three volumes of short stories. His work is performed world-wide, and he has directed his plays in Havana, Stockholm, Munich, Aarhus, Oslo and London.

Henry Livings

Henry Livings started off as an actor, and would start off again if anyone gave him half a chance. It was all a long time ago, but he still remembers the washing-up and the cooking jobs he took in between acting work. He started writing plays for the BBC, and then for the stage; his first to be produced was called *Stop It Whoever You Are* at the Arts Theatre, in London. His plays have been performed all over the world, including New York, Australia and the RNVR Mess Singapore. And he's written two books of short stories: *Pennine Tales* and *Flying Eggs and Things*. Now he lives near Oldham, up the Pennine hills, with a ferret, two lurcher dogs, and a bad cold.

Juliet Ace

I've been a writer for seven years. *A Slight Hitch* was my first play, performed by the Plymouth Theatre Company.

Since then I've written for theatre, radio and television. I've just finished my eleventh episode of *Eastenders*, a week of *Archers* scripts and in between everything I'm working on a radio play for the BBC.

When the ideas run out, I might go back to being a barmaid, an usherette, a teacher, an actor or an auctioneer's clerk. I was a very good barmaid.

Myles Eckersley

Myles Eckersley was born in 1923. He was educated at Marlborough College and Faraday House College of Electrical Engineering, and in the Sergeants' Mess of the Royal Air Force.

After being demobbed he became an art student and graduated as a teacher of Art in 1951. He became the Art teacher at Embley Park School, Romsey, and was in charge of the Drama department.

He has written and produced several plays including *The Ruptured Vulture*, *Orfy in the Underground* and *54321......Implode!* He has also acted in plays; his parts include Fagin in *Oliver* and Feste in *Twelfth Night*.

He has taken early retirement to work on writing and painting.

Joyce Holliday

I've been writing something or other ever since I learned to write at all – poetry, short stories, a novel – but mainly what anybody has wanted to pay me for writing is plays. And, although I've written plays and programmes for radio and television, what I most enjoy is writing for the theatre and a live audience. There is no feeling in the world for me like hearing hundreds of people all laughing together at one of my jokes.

To date I've had twenty-two full-length stage plays produced, on subjects as diverse as hitch-hiking, health care, bull-fighting, and war experiences. In between, I've worked as a secretary, a theatre administrator and a teacher, been married twice and brought up two daughters.

Steve Barlow

Steve Barlow was born in Crewe and educated at Crewe Grammar School, and the Universities of Warwick and Nottingham before joining the teaching profession. After this he decided to find an honest job, and worked for several years in community theatre and Theatre in Education in Nottingham before moving to Norwich to join the DaSilva Puppets. Subsequently he taught English in a village school in Botswana for four years before returning to Nottingham. Steve Barlow is a lecturer at Clarendon College, Nottingham. He lives on the edge of Shipley Park in Derbyshire, and is often to be seen walking around it, muttering darkly.

Steve Skidmore

Steve Skidmore was born in Birstall, Leicester in 1960. He was educated at Longslade College, Birstall, before going to Nottingham University to read English. After graduating, he qualified as a teacher and taught in Nottingham before moving back to Leicester to take up a job as Head of Drama at a Community College.

The plays in the New Plays series are the first he has had published, although he has contributed material for Central TV's award-winning series, *Your Mother Wouldn't Like It*. He has also written a children's book on recycling called *How to Empty a Dustbin*.

Apart from teaching and writing, Steve plays a lot of sport, especially hockey. He can be seen with his battered hockey-stick playing for Leicester Westleigh and Leicestershire every weekend!

ACTIVITIES

How to Write a Play

by Peter Terson

The purpose of this play is to show that practically anyone can write a play, and that the technical mumbo-jumbo that is sometimes used by writers to explain what they do is not nearly as complicated as it sounds. So, how do you go about writing a play? Here are some ideas to get you started.

Instant acting

Instant acting is a technique which requires no preparation. Members of the group are given a situation and must take on their characters, with no rehearsal.
Here are two warm-up exercises for you to attempt.

Directions

Find a partner, call yourself **A** and **B**. **A** has to explain to **B** how to get from a certain place to another place, for example, from the railway station to the town hall. **B** has repeatedly to interrupt with questions and sow as much confusion as possible. How far can **A** take **B** along the route in two minutes? Reverse the roles.

Just a minute

A has to get somewhere urgently; **B** has something very important to tell **A** that can't wait. Play out this situation. Reverse the roles.

Starters

Now try out these situations and starter lines. Again, work in pairs.

CHARACTERS	A brother and a sister.
SETTING	A lounge.
STARTER LINE	Where's my record?

CHARACTERS	A spy and a stranger.
SETTING	A park bench.
STARTER LINE	The sun is red in the East.

CHARACTERS	A tramp and a rich person.
SETTING	A railway station
STARTER LINE	Lend us a quid for a cuppa.

CHARACTERS	Two friends.
SETTING	A classroom.
STARTER LINE	You'll never guess what I heard!

You could extend these scenes by introducing more characters. Invent more scenes with your own characters and settings and act them out.

Consequences game

This is based on the old parlour game, consequences. Each member of the group (ideally around four people) has, in turn, to write the name of a character and one line of dialogue on a piece of paper folded concertina fashion so that no one knows what anyone else has written. You might end up with:

LADY CYNTHIA FITZMELON The petunias are blooming this year.

CAPTAIN KIRK There are Klingons coming at me from all sides. Beam me up Scotty!

WYATT TWERP There ain't room enough for you and me in this town, stranger!

FATHER CHRISTMAS Merry Christmas! Ho Ho Ho!

The challenge is to make up a play around this dialogue. You can have as many other characters as you like and as much additional dialogue as you wish, but these four characters and their lines must be included and make sense in the context of the play.

Any of the above ideas could be used to help you write a play. However, plays usually need more specific planning than instant acting allows. When we work on a prepared theme or with a specific end in mind, we call this an *improvisation*.

Building a play

You can start improvisations from several points. Here are two starting points for you to work from. Work in groups of about five people.

Character

First choose a character. (eg, a zoo keeper, a bank clerk, a nun)
Decide what the character wants. (eg, to stop a toothache, to change jobs, to catch a train)
Decide how the character is to achieve this. (This will be your plot.)

Decide who will help or hinder your character along
the way. (These will be your other characters.)
Give these characters personalities and motivations for
what they do.
Does your character succeed? (This will be your
conclusion.)

Plot

Now start with plot.
*A man is standing on the balcony of a hotel. A woman
joins him. They talk but are interrupted by a noise in
the room. Another man has entered; he has a gun. The
woman leaves with the gunman.*
Who are these people? Why do they do what they do?
Develop these characters and their motivations.

You may not wish to start from plot or character; you
may choose to start from a setting, a theme or an
object. The choice is yours!
You will find that all of these elements are interlinked
and it is usually difficult to isolate one from the others.

From these examples you will see that when you start
to write a play, you don't have to sit down and gaze at
a blank piece of paper (sometimes with a mind to
match!). You can make a tape or video-recording of an
improvisation and write your script from the result.

Extra scenes

What do you think of the way that Peter Terson
completes this play? Could you improvise or write a
different ending to the play?
Nothing much happens in the play. There is very little
action. Improvise a scene in which Ian falls into the
water and is almost drowned. You could add more

characters to rescue him. Where would you put this
scene in the play? Would the new scene make the play
better or would it break up the structure of the play
and spoil it?
Improvise the scene between the girl and the tough. Do
they resolve their problems or not?

Interpretation

In *How to Write a Play* Colin and Ian appear to be
'improvising' around the idea of writing a play, but
they also seem to be unaware of what they are doing.
We call this *dramatic irony*, because the audience
knows more than the characters on stage.

What requirements does Colin say you need for a play?
How are these requirements met as the play develops?
Plays are usually written for a reason. Writers often
disguise their message in order to be more entertaining
and avoid preaching. It is up to us to find clues in the
text in order to decide what the writer's message is. We
call this *interpretation*.

Here are some points of interpretation for you to
discuss:
Colin keeps interrupting the story Ian tells about
maggots. What are we being told here about the
process of writing a play?
Not much happens in the play. How does Peter Terson
keep our interest?
Right at the start, there is tension between Colin and
Ian. What does it consist of? How does it develop
throughout the play?
As the play progresses, we get an idea of the characters
of Colin and Ian. Their characters are shown in
particularly sharp contrast by the dialogue with the

tough. What do we learn of their characters during this exchange?

On page 11 referring to the story he and Colin tell of his family, Ian says 'that's not drama'. Isn't it? Explain your answer.
During your discussion, you may find yourselves disagreeing over some of these points. This is because texts may be interpreted in different ways; there is not a 'correct' answer.

Further reading

It is not always necessary for a play to be full of action. Samuel Beckett explored this idea in *Waiting For Godot*, a play about two tramps who are waiting for a person called Godot to show up. Very little happens in the way of action but, despite this, Beckett keeps the interest of the audience.
Plays need not have a beginning, a middle or an end. The characters need not always know what is going on. Read *Rozencrantz and Guildenstern are Dead* by Tom Stoppard for an example of this idea.
For a different viewpoint on writing plays, read *God (A Play)* by Woody Allen in his book *Without Feathers* (Sphere).

Little Old Lady

by Arnold Wesker

Although smoking on underground trains has been banned for some time, most people thought of this as a rule made for the convenience of non-smokers rather than a necessary safety regulation. This perception changed after the King's Cross disaster.

In this play, Arnold Wesker is concerned with the
Little Old Lady standing up to the Unpleasant Man on
a point of principle: a question of right or wrong. It is a
problem which goes beyond the question of whether
the Unpleasant Man should or should not be allowed
to smoke on the tube train. How do you think the
tragedy at King's Cross affects the way we read and
interpret this play?

Character

Sam, Tracy and Jason are given names: the Little Old
Lady, the Unpleasant Man and the Harassed Woman
are not. Can you suggest a reason for this?

Hot seating

This is a technique which allows us to question the
characters and so find out more about them. The
person playing the character we wish to question must
answer *in role*, that is, in the role of that character.
Suppose we wished to hot seat Sam and Tracy. The
members of the group playing those parts might
answer the questions asked by the rest of the group like
this:

CLASS Hello.
SAM Hello.
TRACY Hi.
CLASS How did you feel when the Old Lady
　　interrupted your conversation on the train?
TRACY I thought it was a bit of a cheek at first, so I was
　　cheeky back. But then I thought she was interesting.
SAM Yeah, not like the old dears who keep telling you
　　how old they are. Sharp, like. She knew a lot – all
　　that stuff about Constantiwotsit . . .

TRACY Nople.

SAM Yeah, and all those capitals.

CLASS When that man started smoking and she asked him to stop, how did you feel?

SAM Well, she had a point.

TRACY Yeah, he had no right.

CLASS But you didn't support her. Why not?

TRACY Well, it was embarrassing. Anyway, it wasn't anything to do with us. If she wanted to stop him, it was up to her.

SAM I reckon that's a bit mean – she was alright. I'd've stuck up for her.

TRACY Oh yes, Superman? Why didn't you then?

SAM Well, I didn't want to start any aggravation while I was with you, did I?

TRACY Why not?

SAM Well, if there'd've been a fight, you might have got hurt.

TRACY Oh, thanks a lot! My hero!

CLASS What if he'd actually hit her?

SAM Oh, I'd've belted him then.

TRACY 'Course you would.

SAM I would!

CLASS But actually, you didn't do anything.

SAM Well, like I said, she was right – but it wasn't that important. Was it?

There may well be other questions you wish to ask Tracy and Sam, and you can question other characters in the same way. You could use the hot seating technique in order to help you answer some of the following questions.

(A further example of hot seating can be found in the exercises on *The Pressure Cooker* on pages 176–7.)

Exploring character

The Little Old Lady describes herself as 'an interfering old woman'. Why does she do this?
Is it an accurate assessment?
Why does she interrupt the conversation between Sam and Tracy?
From what the Little Old Lady says to the Unpleasant Man, does she object to his smoking because she thinks it is dangerous, or is she annoyed because he is breaking the rules.

Sam and Tracy are quite similar in character if not in knowledge.
Why do you think they do not support the Little Old Lady in her argument?
What is their reaction to the argument?

Jason's response is different to Sam and Tracy's. How does it differ?

The Unpleasant Man is really a one-dimensional character. There seems to be little to him other than aggression and spite. Can you detect any other clues to his character?

Exercise

During the argument between the Little Old Lady and the Unpleasant Man, the other characters obviously have their own thoughts. What are they *really* thinking?
Two people, **A** and **B**, sit on chairs. They say nothing.
C and D sit opposite them.
C speaks A's secret thoughts: D speaks B's secret thoughts.
C and D may make up these thoughts or may take their

cues from the way **A** and **B** sit, move and look.

For example, **A** and **B** could be:

An interviewer and interviewee seeking a job.

A shop assistant and customer buying an article of clothing.

A teacher and pupil giving an excuse for being late.

Extra scenes

Why do you think that the Unpleasant Man is so aggressive?

Thinking about this question may not help our understanding of the play, but it will help whoever is playing the part to characterize the role more convincingly.

Is the Unpleasant Man merely a nasty person or has something happened to put him in a bad mood? Perhaps he has had a row with his boss or his wife, or he might have lost a lot of money or had something stolen. Improvise scenes from the Unpleasant Man's day to explain his behaviour.

The Man says at one point '. . . you think yourself lucky you're an old woman'. Improvise your own version of the conflict, but in place of the Little Old Lady, make the objector someone who is as physically strong as the Unpleasant Man.

Arnold Wesker finishes the play as the Little Old Lady pulls the communication cord. Improvise a scene in which you explore what happens next.

Interpretation

Can the Unpleasant Man hear Jason's speech? (page 29) How would he react if he could?

Play this scene twice: first assuming he doesn't hear it;

second, that he does. What difference does this make
to the scene?

Group discussion

Tracy says of teachers that they 'Got no time to teach
us – too busy getting us through exams.' Later she
explains what she means. Do you think this criticism is
a fair one?

The Little Old Lady makes a stand on moral principle.
She believes it is very important that the law should be
obeyed. She faces the danger of being hit by the man if
she doesn't back down. She ignores Jason's warning
that the man might be violent. She also ignores the
possible consequences of stopping the train and the
Harassed Woman's plea not to inconvenience
anybody.

Is the Little Old Lady right in refusing to back down?
Is she being inconsiderate towards the other
passengers? If you think that she is, is she being more
or less inconsiderate than the Man?
Do you admire her courage or think she is being
stubborn over nothing?

If you believe in a moral point, should you ever go
against what you believe or allow someone else to go
against what you believe just in order to stop
inconveniencing others? You might not interfere with
someone smoking in a prohibited area, but would you
interfere when you saw an old lady being mugged?

Can you select any character in the play and say 'That
person is in the right'?

Task

In small groups arrange our laws in an order of merit, with unauthorised smoking at the bottom and murder at the top.
Decide how serious a crime should be before it is punishable.
Which crimes should be punishable by imprisonment.
Should there be a greater deterrent than jail?

Project

People who stick to their beliefs no matter what can suffer great hardship. Some people even die for their beliefs: we call these Martyrs.
Find out about the following people:
    Galileo Galilei
    Sir Thomas More
    Mahatma Gandhi
    Nelson Mandela

Is there any person you particularly admire for standing up for their beliefs?

Debate

Little Old Lady is not concerned with the question of whether smoking is good or bad for you; rather, it questions the individual's right to smoke where and when they please.

Organize a debate with the motion 'Smoking should be banned.'
In a formal debate, one person proposes a motion and speaks in its favour.
They are then opposed by another speaker.

A 'second' then adds their views supporting the motion and is opposed by a fourth speaker.

The chairperson then asks members of the audience for their comments.
The principal speakers are then allowed to sum up their arguments and a vote is taken to decide who has given the best argument.

Further reading

Another play which deals with a moral principle is *An Enemy of the People* by Henrik Ibsen. It is set in a small town whose spa waters become polluted. The setting provides the background for a battle between Dr Stockmann who wishes to close the spa on health grounds, and the greedy and corrupt officials who do not wish to lose any money.
(This is also the dilemma that faces the hero of the film *Jaws*.)

The story of Sir Thomas More can be read in *A Man For All Seasons* by Robert Bolt. More was beheaded after refusing to betray his religious beliefs. *The Life of Galileo* by Bertolt Brecht follows the story of the Italian astronomer who was persecuted for stating that the Earth was NOT at the centre of the universe. The Catholic church made Galileo take back this statement threatening him with death if he did not. Galileo took back his statement, declaring 'Grub before ethics'.

The Great Camel Rumbles and Groans and Spits

by Henry Livings

This is a very different play from the others in the anthology. It is based on a folk-tale from Africa. People have been telling each other such stories since Man first learnt to speak. Sometimes these stories explain how the world was created or why things have come to be as they are. Other stories teach lessons about life and so make a point or illustrate a moral. Aesop's fables fall into this category.

For thousands of years, these stories were not written down: they were passed on by word of mouth by storytellers, bards or minstrels and families. The stories tend to be simple so that they can be remembered, repetitious so that the audience can join in at certain points and entertaining in order to keep the audience interested.

Dramatization

In *The Great Camel* Henry Livings has taken a story, not originally written for the stage, and has turned it into a play. This is known as dramatization.
Here is another folk-tale, told by the Tswana tribe from Southern Africa:

> All the birds were invited to a feast in the sky, by the Sky Spirit. They were very pleased and chattered about the great occasion. Tortoise heard them, and being a very greedy animal, wanted to go too. He begged and pleaded until the birds agreed to carry him to the Sky Spirit's palace.
> While they were preparing for the flight, Tortoise

told the birds that for such an important occasion, they should give themselves grand-sounding names. The birds were struck with this idea, and started inventing impressive titles for each other. Then they asked Tortoise what names he had chosen. He replied, 'I shall call myself, "All of You".' The birds laughed. They thought Tortoise had chosen a very dull name.

When they reached the palace of the Sky Spirit, they found a magnificent feast set out for them. They were all announced by their splendid new names; but before they could begin the feast, Tortoise stood up and asked who the feast was for.

'Why, for all of you,' replied the Sky Spirit.

'All of You!' cried Tortoise. 'That's me!' And he set to and gobbled up all of the food.

The birds were furious at this trick, and refused to carry Tortoise back to Earth. In any case, they said, he was too heavy after eating all of the food that was meant for everyone. Tortoise pleaded with the birds to help him, but they would not listen. However, the last bird to leave, an Egret, offered to take a message to Tortoise's wife.

'Tell her,' said Tortoise, 'to fetch all the rugs and mattresses and cushions and soft things out of the house, and make a pile in the middle of my garden, for me to fall on.'

The Egret went to Tortoise's wife, but he told her to put all the stones, knives, axes and kettles she could find into a pile. She did so, and Tortoise, who was too far up in the sky to see properly, thought she was obeying his instructions.

So, he jumped and fell to Earth; and when he hit the pile of sharp things his wife had made, his shell cracked into many pieces. His wife took him to the medicine man to be healed and he did not die. But, if you look at a tortoise today, you can still see the cracks in his shell that Tortoise suffered in his fall from the sky.

Dramatize this story. You could improvise the whole of it or select one or two scenes to dramatize.
Henry Livings represents the hump of the camel with an umbrella. How could you represent Tortoise's shell? How would you stage Tortoise's fall from the sky?

Exercise

Improvise a scene in which Tortoise is brought before a court of animals to be tried for his misdeeds.
To help you characterize these animals, first try miming the actions of an animal, for example, a frog, a monkey, a chicken. Pay particular attention to their movements. Are they fast or slow, smooth or jerky? Then think about the characters of the animals. What do they suggest to you? A fox may be cunning, a hippopotamus may be stupid, a monkey may be excitable. Try to combine the physical characteristics and the personality of the animal you choose to represent.

Rituals

In the play, the villagers perform two ritual dances: the Dance of the Hoe, to teach Kilak, and the Hunting Dance before they set off in pursuit of the Great Camel. Many people believe that such rituals were the beginning of theatre.

A ritual takes place on a special occasion and conforms to an accepted set of rules; as Luo says to Kilak, 'Learn the customs'.

Ritual still exists today, for instance, most Saturday afternoons rituals take place at football matches and in churches! We see spectators at a football match clapping, chanting, waving scarves, and perhaps even dancing (jumping up and down), urging their team to win. All of these activities conform to an accepted and familiar pattern. A wedding also has elements of ritual. What are they?

Projects

Ritual is often associated with a particular point in the life of an individual, or of a society. Personal rituals include baptisms, bar-mitzvahs, weddings and funerals. In what rituals do we take part as a society or nation?

Find out about ritual in both primitive and modern times.
Devise a ritual dance, like the Hoe Dance in *The Great Camel*, to instruct a stranger in something important in our daily lives. For example, going shopping, washing pots or even playing golf! Make use of basic rhythms: handclaps, chants, drums and percussion instruments.

Interpretation

Folk tales tend to be very simple. However, we can still find points within the text to discuss and analyse.
Henry Livings uses a narrator (the drummer) to introduce the story. How does this make the playwright's job easier?
Anansi's repetition of the phrase 'She's all three!' allows the audience to join in with her. But each time she says it, she means something different.

What does she mean on each occasion?
What other instances of repetition are there in the
play?
Kilak points out that Chiqui (on page 44) refers to the
fields as hers rather than her husbands. What
significance has this?
What is the point of:
Kilak cooking the feast of the Great Camel?
The resurrection of the Great Camel at the end?

Masks

The staging of *The Great Camel* calls for the making of
masks.
Masks can be made out of many materials: papier-
mâché, card, wood, etc.
They have been used from the earliest times for ritual
dances and drama.
Design and make the masks required for the
production of *The Great Camel*.
You can make them as elaborate or as simple as you
wish.
There are many books on mask-making you can refer
to. Ask your librarian.

Further reading

You can read more African folk tales in *Myths and
Legends of the Swahili* by Jan Knappert, published by
Heinemann.

European folk-tales were made very popular by Hans
Christian Anderson and the Brothers Grimm. There
are many books which include their stories.
The rituals that occur at football matches form part of
Peter Terson's superb play, *Zigger Zagger*.

A Slight Hitch

by Juliet Ace

A Slight Hitch captures a moment in the lives of three unrelated people.

Their only connection is that they are all 'on the road'. There is no definite beginning or conclusive ending to the play. It is like a snapshot, capturing a moment in time.

A previous play in the anthology, *Little Old Lady*, seeks to make a moral point, or at least, a point about morals; whereas *A Slight Hitch* shows the characters as they are. It makes no judgements.

Instant acting

Choose a location in which people meet by chance: a railway station, a park bench, a plane. Two members of the group begin. They choose their own characters. They meet and fall into conversation. Other characters enter the scene as they wish. Make sure that not too many characters are involved at any one time. Can such a scene ever end or is it like *A Slight Hitch* in the sense that it has no definite ending? How close is this situation to real life?

Character

To help us discover more about the play, it would be helpful to explore the thoughts and feelings of the characters. We can do this by using the technique of hot seating.

Hot seating

Ask the people playing the characters questions which

they must answer in role. This technique is described in the extension work for *Little Old Lady* on page 151. Concentrate on what they think of each other, what Josie thinks about Lindy and vice versa and what Gina thinks of the other two.

Jason is mentioned but never appears. Give a member of the group this role and ask him what he thinks of the two girls.

How do we react to the characters? What are your feelings towards them?

Extra scenes

Because *A Slight Hitch* deals with one particular moment, you may wish to add extra scenes to it in order to develop and explore the play further.

Here are some suggestions for extra scenes you may wish to consider:

   The scene in which Josie has the argument with her mother.
   The scene where Lindy meets Jason, the lorry driver.
   A scene in which Lindy and Jason talk about having left Josie behind.
   A scene in which Josie's mother goes to the police.
   A scene in which Josie goes home.

Perhaps Josie doesn't go home: does she learn to survive on the road?

Improvise some scenes which explore this idea.

Interpretation

Lindy immediately disappears at the beginning of the play and does not reappear until later. However, we are constantly aware of her presence. How does Juliet Ace achieve this?

Group discussion

Nearly everyone has an argument at home with parents, guardians, brothers and sisters. Many people threaten to leave home. Have any people in your group ever threatened to leave home? Why?
Did they actually run away? What happened?

The Samaritans and, more recently, Childline, provide a valuable counselling and listening service. Every year they receive thousands of calls from people who want to, or have, run away from home. They have to have special skills in dealing with people on the telephone. Try the following exercise:

'Can I help you . . .?'

Find a partner. Nominate yourselves **A** and **B**. Sit with your backs to each other. **A** makes up a problem that is worrying them, for example, they have just fallen out with their best friend.

B has to discover what the problem is by asking questions. However, **A** cannot talk. They can only answer by tapping: one tap for no, two for yes.
When **B** has discovered the problem, they give their advice to **A**.
When this has been completed, discuss the advice given and then swap roles.

Project

The Beatles' song 'She's Leaving Home' from the *Sergeant Pepper* album is both famous and very evocative. Use this to either:

Produce a piece of dance-drama or movement-to-music, with the girl miming her actions. Include

the reactions of her parents and the meeting with
'the man from the motor trade'.

or: Produce a series of slide photographs, using actual
locations (the house, a bus station, a garage, etc.)
to be accompanied by the music.

or: If you have access to the equipment, produce a
videotape, using the music as a soundtrack.

Are there any other pieces of music you could use to
explore the theme of leaving home?

Role play

In this type of exercise, every member of the group
takes on a role, that is, takes the part of another
person. A situation is agreed upon, and the members of
the group then act as their characters would. This type
of simulation is called role play.

Josie has disappeared. She has left a note saying
farewell. In the group, decide what Josie would say in
the letter.
There is to be an inquiry by social services. Choose
someone to be in charge of the inquiry. The rest of the
group take on roles of people who are connected with
Josie in some way. They could be family, friends,
neighbours or teachers. Choose your own role.
Interview everyone: can they throw any light on Josie's
disappearance? You might like to improvise some of
the scenes, for example, the scene where Josie talks
about leaving home to a friend. The possibilities are
endless.

Further reading

Read *The Pressure Cooker* on page 102. Compare the
pressures on Josie with those on Andrea. Like *Little*

Old Lady (page 19), *A Slight Hitch* explores the idea
of characters being brought together by chance.
Disaster movies like *Airport* or *The Towering Inferno*
also have this as a starting point – people thrown
together by chance.

Slave!

by Myles Eckersley

Slave! is a different type of play from the others in the
book. We are not concerned with the characters, we
are more concerned with the subject matter. In the
course of the play, we may feel sympathy for Edward,
but is it because we like him as a person or because he
is a victim of slavery?

Interpretation

Myles Eckersley has three main aims in *Slave*:
1 To entertain us.
2 To give us background information about the times
   in which slavery flourished.
3 To show us the facts and outcome of an actual case,
   which helped in the abolition of slavery.

How successful is he in achieving these aims?
As in *The Great Camel* (page 33), this play uses a
narrator. Oats is clearly anti-slavery. Would it make a
difference if the narrator was for slavery? How would
it change the 'feel' of the play if Lord Somersett was
the narrator?

Much of the play is set in the court room, but a lengthy
section in the middle tells us of Edward's past life. This
technique of 'going back' is called *flashback*. How
would you stage these scenes?

How does Myles Eckersley gain sympathy for Edward
and make Lord Somerset and the judge look stupid?
What is Sir Granville's *real* motive in taking on
Edward's defence?

Group discussion

We think of slavery as Europeans transporting
Africans to the West Indies and America to work on
the plantations in the eighteenth and nineteenth
centuries. However, many other races were enslaving
each other hundreds of years before this. A prisoner of
war in Ancient Greece became a slave and Plato, the
greatest Greek philosopher, could not imagine a
society without slaves. In Roman times, slaves were an
accepted part of society: thieves were made to row in
the galleys or fight as gladiators in the circuses.

There are many forms of slavery. After the abolition of
slavery in America, many of the freed slaves were
worse off. As slaves they were prized possessions,
worth hundreds or thousands of dollars each: as
unattached workers they were paid as little as their
bosses could get away with and also had to find their
keep.

Piece-work is a type of work where a worker is paid
for the amount of things they make. Seasonal work,
like fruit and vegetable picking, is also paid on a
productivity basis. Is there any similarity between
these forms of work and slavery?

Project

Find out about migratory work, such as that
performed by black mineworkers in South Africa. Why
do they leave their homes in the independent states to

work in the mines of South Africa?
Discuss your findings. Put yourself in the
mineworkers' place. What would you do?

Extra scenes

A person is very unhappy at work. They long to leave.
However, they have no other job to go to and are
obviously concerned about unemployment. Improvise
some scenes in that person's life. How does it affect
their social and home lives? Does it make them a
different person, more moody for instance? From these
improvisations could you say that the person is a slave
within their own life?

Role play

This technique, described in the extension work to *A
Slight Hitch* on page 166, is a good way in which to
explore a historical situation in such a way that
everyone is involved.

Read the following outline of the villagers of Eyam.
You can add your own research material to it as well.
   During the plague of London a bundle of cloth was
   sent to the Derbyshire village of Eyam from a
   supplier in London in 1665.
   Unfortunately, the cloth contained plague-carrying
   fleas in it and soon villagers began to die of the
   plague.
   Because the plague was highly contagious, the
   villagers, led by the rector William Mompesson,
   decided to put their whole village in quarantine,
   despite the fact that they would probably die if they
   stayed in Eyam. Many of the villagers died but their
   heroic act meant that the plague did not pass on to
   other parts of Derbyshire.

Divide the group into families in Eyam. Decide on your characters. What is your trade? Are you married? What are your thoughts on the fact that you could die?

Once you have decided your character, hold a meeting to decide what is to be done about the outbreak of plague. Is your group's decision similar to that of the villagers of Eyam?

You might wish to script or *document* your results. If you do, you will have produced a play of the same type as *Slave!*, a drama-documentary. You could research your own facts for such a play: it could involve a nationally-known historical incident, for example, The Peasants Revolt of 1381, or you could choose an incident of local interest.

Perhaps the most famous and most frequently performed example of historical drama-documentary is *Oh, What A Lovely War!*

A good example of a local subject is *The Knotty* by Peter Cheeseman and the company of the Victoria Theatre, Stoke on Trent. It deals with the history of a relatively unimportant local railway.

Further reading

There are many books on the subject of slavery, both factual and fictional. Mark Twain's *Huckleberry Finn* contains a moving account of Huck's relationship with Nigger Jim, who he comes to recognize as a human being and not merely a slave. *Flash for Freedom* by George MacDonald Fraser contains many excellent descriptions of the slave trade in America.

A Message From the Other Side

by Joyce Holliday

Nearly everyone has invited friends round to their house when parents are out. Parties are arranged to coincide when parents are on holiday or away for the evening, and the evidence is quickly cleaned up before they return. However, brothers and sisters may have to be bribed not to tell parents about these goings-on. In *A Message From the Other Side* Michael holds out for two packets of crisps and the chocolate biscuits! Have you ever had to bribe a brother or sister not to let on, or been bribed yourself not to say anything by your brother or sister?

Exercise

Work in pairs. You are brothers or sisters. Your parents are out and one of you wants to invite friends round for a party. You have two minutes to persuade the other to let you have the party and not tell your parents.
After two minutes, reverse the roles.
As a group, discuss the types of persuasion you used. Was it bribery? Was it threatening? What sort of things did you promise?
Do you use such tactics in real life?

Role play

Choose three people in the group to be members of a family. Two of the people chosen are parents, the other is their son or daughter. The rest of the group are friends of the son/daughter.
The parents are going out for the evening. Unknown to

them, their son/daughter has arranged a party and
invited friends round.
Improvise the scene in which the parents are getting
ready to go out.
The parents go just as people begin to arrive.
Improvise the party. In the middle of it, the parents
return. Improvise what happens.

Character

Joyce Holliday gives a brief description of the
characters before the play begins. Do these
descriptions help you to understand the characters? Do
you think they are interesting characters?
Choose three of the characters and write a description,
fully describing their personalities.

Extra scenes

Do you find the ending of the play satisfactory or do
you find Mrs Proctor's appearance a disappointment?
Improvise or script a different ending to the play.
Improvise or script a scene in which Mrs Proctor tells
Sarah's mother about the beer.

What would happen if the séance really worked?
Improvise or script such a scene.

Touch sensitivity

The characters in *A Message From the Other Side* find
it difficult to guess who is moving the glass. Try this
exercise to see how difficult it is to spot such
movement:
Two people face each other, touching only with their
fingertips. They agree who is to lead and who is to
follow. The leader, using the lightest possible pressure,

guides the follower through a series of movements. These could include moving up and down or around the room.

If this is done well, an observer should not be able to tell who is leading and who is following.

Interpretation

A Message From the Other Side takes the supernatural as its theme. Many people take this subject very seriously, but Joyce Holliday treats it light-heartedly, without making fun of it. What did you find funny in the play?

Séances are considered to be very dangerous by some people. This allows Joyce Holliday to use the possible dangers of the séance to build up a series of moments of high drama, or climaxes. She then releases the tension so that we return, once again, from the supernatural to the everyday. Where do these climaxes come and how is the tension released?

Other plays in this anthology have dramatic climaxes: read *Little Old Lady* or *The Pressure Cooker* and identify where these moments occur.

Consider a television series like *Star Trek* or *Cagney and Lacey*. How often do dramatic climaxes occur in these programmes? Is there a pattern and, if so, why are these moments deliberately spaced out?

Projects

Many people believe in the supernatural. Find out about clairvoyants, fortune-tellers, mediums and other such people.

Many people visit this type of person to have their futures told. They have their palms read, their tarot cards interpreted and even their tea leaves looked at. What other forms of fortune-telling are there?

Astrology

Thousands of people read their stars every day. The stars are printed in papers, magazines and books and are read on television and radio.
Collect as many astrological forecasts for one day as you can. Do they all forecast the same things? Are they specific in their predictions, or could they have more than one meaning?
What sort of things do they predict? Make a list of these.
Make up tomorrow's horoscope for a friend. Do the things actually happen?

Further reading

The Ghost Train by Arnold Ridley, is old-fashioned, melodramatic and a lot of fun, as is *Gaslight* by Patrick Hamilton. There are hundreds of ghost stories and the better ones can be found in popular anthologies.
Magic and ghosts are common in many of Shakespeare's plays: *Macbeth, A Midsummer Nights Dream* and *The Tempest* are full of supernatural goings-on.

The Pressure Cooker

by Steve Barlow and Steve Skidmore

Arguments

Everybody has had an argument at some time. We argue with family, friends, teachers and even complete strangers. Sometimes these can lead to serious situations. In the heat of the argument, we may say something we don't mean to, or lose our control and begin to fight.

Do you think that the argument between Andrea and her mother is typical?

What do you argue about most of all?

Try out the following exercise, to see how arguments can develop:

Verbal boxing

Two people sit opposite each other.

They are given a situation to argue about. For example, one has borrowed an article of clothing from the other, without asking permission.

They have one minute to argue about the situation.

At the end of the minute, the rest of the group vote on who has given the best argument. The group should vote for the person who gives the best constructed argument not the loudest one!

The winner stays on, and a new challenger and new situation is presented.

No bad language or threats to punch the other one are allowed. If this happens the person is disqualified.

Extra scenes

This play was deliberately written in an episodic style in order for you to develop it and explore issues which you may feel relevant. The end is left open for you to decide what is to happen to Andrea.

Here are some suggestions for further scenes you may wish to develop and explore.

The play ends with the ringing of the telephone. Who

could be ringing? Is it news about Andrea? If so, is it good or bad? Continue the last scene with Ian answering the phone.

A scene in which Dawn tells Graham what Andrea has done.
A scene in which something else goes wrong in Andrea's life. Where might you insert such a scene in the play as it stands?

A scene in which Andrea, having survived the overdose, sees Dawn for the first time.

A scene in which Andrea's mother informs Andrea's father of the overdose. There are many other scenes you could improvise, in order to gain a greater understanding of the characters and situations. What others would you wish to explore?

Hot seating

Hot seating can help us to understand the characters and reasons for their actions. The technique can also be used to gain different perspectives of the play. Here is another useful example of how this can work. Suppose we decided that Andrea survived the overdose and that we wished to question the mother about the incident. The girl playing the mother might answer the questions of the class like this.

CLASS Hello.

MOTHER Hello.

CLASS Could we ask your name?

MOTHER Shirley. Shirley Brooks.

CLASS It must have been a terrible experience.

MOTHER Yes. I couldn't believe it. I didn't think Andrea was so silly.

CLASS Silly?

MOTHER Taking an overdose, like that. She was very lucky I found her.

CLASS You found her?

MOTHER Yes in her room. On the bed. There was an empty bottle of tablets. They were my sleeping pills. I've been taking them for years. Ever since my husband left me. I just didn't believe that she'd do something like this. Lucky I was there to call the ambulance.

CLASS Why did she do it, has she said?

MOTHER No I don't know. Ask her. We'd had a row but we've had them before.

CLASS What do you row about.

MOTHER Everything! She's going through a difficult period. Boys, exams. She wants to go to university, you know. I think she misses her father. That might be it.

CLASS Why did he leave?

MOTHER I'd rather not talk about it.

CLASS You told Andrea that it was her fault that he left.

MOTHER Did I? Well, yes, I suppose it was, partly. I don't want to talk about it.

CLASS Do you prefer Ian or Andrea?

MOTHER I love them both.

CLASS But do you have a favourite?

MOTHER Of course not. Ian's different to Andrea. I love them both. Although Ian never did anything like this.

CLASS What will happen now?

MOTHER Well, it takes time, doesn't it? Andrea's going to stay with my ex-husband for a while. It'll help her get away. Let her get things in order.

CLASS What then?

MOTHER I don't know, I haven't thought about it.

Each person has their own viewpoint. Andrea's mother still thinks that Andrea wishes to go to university. Her view is totally different from her daughter's. They have a different perception of the situation. Hot seating can help us to become aware of these different perceptions and so help our understanding of situations and experiences.

Who else would help you to gain a different perspective? You may wish to hot seat characters who don't appear in the play, for example, a school teacher, Andrea's father. These could give us a different perspective of the situation.

Interpretation

All of these different perspectives need to be interpreted. For example, why doesn't Andrea's mother want her to go to Drama College? Who do we believe when Andrea says that Ian is the favourite and her mother says that neither is? Would it help to ask the father or Ian, or would this only confuse the issue even more? We have to use the clues and our own experiences in order to interpret the situation correctly. Is there ever a correct interpretation? Is life as simple as that?

Interpretation is also needed when we use a play text. There are many different ways of interpreting the way characters should say lines.
In Scene 3 Andrea's last word is 'Nobody'. This could be said in a variety of ways: screamed at Graham as an accusation, or, perhaps, said very quietly to herself, so that Graham cannot hear her. Which way would you use? Would you use another way? If so, why?
By experimenting with different interpretations, we can come to a better understanding of problems. We

take clues and put them together to create a solution.

One of the clues in the play is the title, *The Pressure Cooker*. Why do you think it is called this? Do you think this is a good title? If not, what would you call the play?

Exercises

Everyone is put under pressure at some point in their lives. Different people react to it in different ways. Who do you turn to in a crisis? Discuss this with the group. Does the person you turn to depend on what the problem is?

Agony aunts

Andrea writes to an agony aunt for advice on her problems. Write the reply you think 'Emily' would have given.
Write a letter to an agony aunt.
Swap it with another person.
Write a reply to the other person's problem.
Return the advice and discuss it with that person.

Project

Collect agony aunt columns from newspapers and magazines.
Make a survey of the problems that people write in about.
Put these problems into categories, for example, health, family, boy-friends, girl-friends, money, etc.
What are the most common problems?
Do the same problems in different magazines receive the same advice?

Diary

Write a diary for Andrea based on the events of the play. Include the note that she left before she took the overdose.

Further reading

Another play in the anthology also deals with family pressure. Read *A Slight Hitch* to compare how the characters react differently to Andrea.

The Weeping Madonna

by Peter Terson

Peter Terson has told this story in the form of a verse drama. It was normal for playwrights to write plays in verse from the earliest times. Greek and Roman plays dating from as long ago as 500 BC were written in verse. This tradition continued until the eighteenth century, when verse drama fell into disuse. Occasionally, a modern playwright will attempt a verse drama. Verse drama occurs on British stages every year at Christmas, when people flock to see a traditional pantomime.

Interpretation

Why do you think Peter Terson chose to write the play in verse?
Do you like this form of writing?
Select a scene from the play. Rewrite it or improvise it using everyday speech. How does this affect the length and atmosphere of the scene?
It is obvious that rhymes like:

I shan't ask full price, not half or quarter,
  I'll crucify myself, more than I oughta . . .

are not to be taken seriously. What other intentionally
bad rhymes can you find in the play?

Another device used by Peter Terson is *irony*. This is
where he uses words that suggest one meaning but, in
fact, mean something totally the opposite. For
example:

MRS FORD It will be as secret with us as if we'd never
  heard.
NARRATOR And so the news was spread from mouth to
  mouth.

What does Peter Terson imply here? What does it tell
us about the character of Mrs Ford?
What other instances of irony appear in the play?

Staging

Try staging a scene with the characters acting as they
would in real life. Now try staging the scene again,
only this time, overact: talk directly to the audience,
exaggerate your movements and emphasise your
words. In short, play it like a pantomime.
Which way suits the scene better?

Character

The characters in *The Weeping Madonna* are generally
one dimensional. Melanie is the most realistic, but
most of the others are caricatures. They are not
realistic people, but rather are representatives of
attitudes found in society, for example, the council
officials and the policeman.
Why does everyone 'jump on the bandwagon' and help

spread the fame of the Madonna? What changes their minds about the statue?
Do you think Melanie is right to destroy the Madonna?

Exercises

Introduce more 'hangers-on'. For example, a schoolteacher, a social worker, a TV documentary producer. How would you caricature these figures of society?

You are a reporter. You hear of the miracle of the Madonna. Produce a front page story. Interview the various characters. If possible, tape or video the interviews and produce a radio or television news item.

Melanie buys the Madonna from a market salesman. Each member of the group brings in a worthless or hideous object and attempts to auction it off to the others.

Group discussion

On finding Melanie on her knees before the Madonna, her mother says:
    Oh God don't give her religion . . .
    What a disease . . .

This seems to be quite a common attitude today, not so much fear of religion but embarrassment whenever it is mentioned. Why do you think this is?

The miracle of the Weeping Madonna causes outrage and worship. Why do you think miracles arouse such violent feelings?
Would you ever believe in a miracle?
What would you describe as being the main themes of the play?

Projects

Find out about any miracles that are reputed to have occurred in your region of the country. Can you explain any of them, or do you, like Melanie, 'not want proof'?

Write a verse drama. Think of a simple plot, a fairy story or nursery rhyme, for example. If you wish to attempt a larger scale verse drama, you could use the following plot:

> Grandfather falls out of a tree and breaks his neck. His grandchildren are relieved as they thought he was a wicked, old person, mean and bad tempered. Their parents tell them not to speak ill of the dead and say how good he was.
>
> However, when the will is read, it is discovered that grandfather has left all his money to a donkey sanctuary, as donkeys have more sense than people. This causes the parents to complain bitterly about the old man, while the children begin to realise how lonely he must have been and feel sorry for him.

Further reading

If you would like to explore some other verse dramas, try looking at some examples of medieval mystery and miracle plays. Also look at the morality plays which followed, particularly *Everyman*.